In Loving Memory

of

Mikey

2010

Dear Mary

Getting Lucky

Reverence for All Life

Namaste

Susan

Getting

Lucky

*How One Special Dog Found Love
and a Second Chance at Angel's Gate*

SUSAN MARINO

FOUNDER OF ANGEL'S GATE ANIMAL HOSPICE

with Denise Flaim

Stewart, Tabori & Chang
New York

Published in 2005 by
Stewart, Tabori & Chang
An imprint of Harry N. Abrams, Inc.

Copyright © 2005 Susan Marino
Illustrations copyright © 2005 Kathleen Edwards
Angel's Gate song by Lori Carlson

Library of Congress Cataloging-in-Publication Data
Marino, Susan.
    Getting lucky : the story of Angel's Gate Animal Hospice / Susan Marino with
Denise Flaim.
       p.   m.
ISBN-13: 978-1-58479-410-3
ISBN-10: 1-58479-410-0
    1. Dogs—New York—Long Island—Anecdotes. 2. Cats—New York—Long
Island—Anecdotes. 3. Pets—New York—Long Island—Anecdotes. 4. Angel's Gate
Animal Hospice—Anecdotes. 5. Marino, Susan. I. Flaim, Denise. II. Title.
SF426.2.M355 2005
636.08'32'0974721—dc22   2004062638

Designed by Laura Lindgren

The text of this book was composed in Stempel Schneidler and Monotype Script.

Printed and bound in the United States of America

10 9 8 7 6 5 4 3

HNA
harry n. abrams, inc.
a subsidiary of La Martinière Groupe
115 West 18th Street
New York, NY 10011
www.hnabooks.com

Contents

Susan

From the street, it looks like a typical suburban ranch house. There's a big green lawn and a hydrangea tree weighed down with blooms turned pink and gold by the frost. There's a chain-link fence around the yard, which has a swimming pool and a deck and an umbrella-topped patio set. Cedar shingles, asphalt-paved driveway. Just ordinary Long Island suburbia.

But there's nothing ordinary going on inside Angel's Gate.

A pack of at least a dozen dogs, a barking jumble of fur in every color, length, and texture, greets visitors at the door. Seemingly oblivious to the canine patrol, cats climb everywhere: on kitchen counters, on windowsills, on your shoulder, a steady purr in your ear. Through a set of French doors, the sunny great room is lined with birdcages, where macaws preen, Quakers nibble fresh veggies, and a sulfur-crested cockatoo lets out an occasional shriek. In the backyard, next to the swimming pool where a paralyzed Doberman might be floating in the middle of a physical-therapy session, a trio of geriatric ponies shares a freshly raked corral with a parade of geese.

Angel's Gate is a first—a residential hospice for animals. It's hard to keep an exact tally, but the head count is always more than a hundred, sometimes two hundred, sometimes even more. For the past decade, Angel's Gate has been a refuge for animals who have no one to care for them—dogs dying of cancer, cats infected with feline AIDS, ponies slated for euthanasia because they could no longer bear the weight of the children who rode them, parrots mutilated in pet-store accidents, squirrels hit by cars and left for dead.

If a creature is broken or dying or damaged, he finds a home here. And Angel's Gate is truly a home. It is my home.

My name is Susan Marino. I dreamed of this place and created it on this little patch of suburbia, which I share with my teenage daughter Dantae, my son Todd, and Victor, my companion of twelve years. My days follow the rhythms of these animals' lives: I give subcutaneous injections of fluid to the cats in renal failure, I slide Brutus, a 165-pound paraplegic Rottweiler, into the hot tub for his daily hydrotherapy sessions. I feed, I mop, I wash soiled linens, and then I mop some more.

I don't believe in crates or cages, and with the exception of the parrots, the animals have free rein. The dogs sleep in our bed, the cats march across our kitchen table. Injured blue jays convalesce in the guest room, a dying cat rests in a playpen draped with an oxygen tent in another bedroom. In addition to getting palliative care in the true tradition of hospice, the animals of Angel's Gate receive a variety of holistic treatments—acupuncture, chiropractic, flower essences, aromatherapy, essential oils, Chinese herbs, and Reiki, to name just a few.

To be sure, I'm no Mother Teresa—at times I feel more like Erin Brockovich, as I host fund-raisers and mail out press releases and try, bit by bit, to make others see the lessons that these animals have taught me: that every life, no matter how limited or how shattered, is worthwhile.

Many of the animals at Angel's Gate have incurable diseases, from cancer to diabetes. Some are just old, worn out from a lifetime spent serving humans whose only thanks was to throw them away. Some are incontinent, or have been paralyzed in accidents or by the inevitability of genetics. Some are neurologically impaired, hobbling and spasming their way through the house's freshly scrubbed hallways.

Yes, they are dying, but they are still alive. And our goal is to let them live out the time they have left with dignity and joy.

For thirty years, I was an intensive-care pediatrics nurse. Nursing has always felt like a warm, comfortable pair of slippers to me. I couldn't imagine doing anything else. It is the one unbroken thread that has followed me through my life, from the stuffed animals I bandaged up as a child to the broken adolescents I tended as a psychiatric-ward nurse. And now, these animals have become my patients and my friends.

Before I left nursing to found Angel's Gate, I earned a six-figure salary. I drove a nice car, had manicured nails and designer clothes. Some people have a hard time understanding why I would walk away from all that to spend my days cleaning out litter boxes and mopping up behind incontinent dogs, living on donations and relying on a small army of volunteers to keep things afloat.

The answer is that it would have been more difficult *not* to. Running Angel's Gate is what I was born to do. It's as simple—and I guess as complicated—as that.

At Angel's Gate contradictions live side by side as easily and as naturally as our cats and dogs. Most of our animals are dying, yet the house brims with life and vitality. Volunteers come to rake leaves, or clean the parrots' cages, or spend some time doling out ear scratches and tummy rubs, and the hours melt away. It's a place where the final stages of life are honored and celebrated, not feared and denied; where the inviolability of nature and her healing powers are respected alongside modern medicine. Here the animals are as much teachers as patients, setting forth life lessons that resonate long after they are gone.

But do they ever really leave? Hundreds of animals have walked or been carried across the sprawling lawn in front of Angel's Gate. And even after their bodies tire and they make the passage to whatever awaits them beyond, for me they never quite go. I feel them in the rustle of the tree branches over the pool, in the glint of sun illuminating the spare bedroom that doubles as a wildlife-rehabilitation room. They become part of the huge shimmering tapestry that Angel's Gate spins, in its quiet, constant way, every day, even as the rest of the world keeps whirling.

Collectively, their stories are the heart and soul of Angel's Gate. Each animal has made a mark, taught an important lesson, or touched a heart. But of all the creatures who have called Angel's Gate home, there was one who encompassed all that we try to do here—to nurture both the body and the spirit, and to restore dignity to life and death.

His name was Lucky.

Lucky

I picked up the ringing phone, a diabetic cat cradled in one hand, Christmas decoration dangling from the other.

It was Christmas Eve 1999, and Vic and I were rushing around to finish our last-minute holiday chores. The ten-foot tree in the great room was still undecorated, and the parrots in the cages lining the room commented periodically with wolf whistles. Vic's presents to the family were sprawled on the dining-room table, where the cats were sabotaging his efforts at wrapping by getting tangled up in the Scotch tape and walking all over the paper. I was cooking up a vegetarian Christmas dinner for our family, which was to assemble the next day.

"Hello, this is the ASPCA," said the voice on the other end of the line. "We have a dog we're wondering if you can take. Tonight."

I listened quietly as the adoption coordinator explained the dog's dire circumstances. He was emaciated, abused, close to death. At fourteen and a half, he was too old to offer for adoption, and his prognosis was too shaky for the ASPCA to invest any more medical resources in him. They did not have the funds to bankroll his recovery, if he could even make one. It was either euthanasia, or Angel's Gate.

By the time I hung up the phone, I wondered why I had said yes. Even if I managed to get through my Christmas to-do list, there were still the daily goings-on at the hospice to attend to. The two cats in renal failure needed subcutaneous injections. Sarah, a Tibetan spaniel and former show dog whose deteriorating spine left her paralyzed and incontinent, had deposited a fresh puddle in the hallway. A few feet away was the door to the bathroom, which was temporary winter lodging for a swan with a broken pelvis who watched with interest whenever someone heeded the call of nature. The tub was overdue for a cleaning, and the whole house needed another pass with the mop, a chore I repeat countless times a day, to keep Angel's Gate smelling clean and fresh.

But deep down, I knew why I had said yes to the call about a hopeless-sounding dog. I said yes because Angel's Gate is the last resort, the last chance; and if any animal sounded like he needed a last chance, it was this one.

I believe in the impossible. If I didn't, I wouldn't have founded Angel's Gate. Starting the hospice took every ounce of strength and determination I had, and not just because of the precarious financial position it put us in. (When you rely on donations to live, money is always tight.) But Angel's Gate also required that I close the door on a life that was comfortable and safe and expected, and step out into the unknown.

I grew up a good Catholic girl on Long Island, and for the first thirty-odd years of my life, I did exactly what my family expected of me: I got a nursing degree, I married at twenty-one, and had four children in short order. My husband never drank, never raised his hand against me, never gave me any reason to complain. I had a beautiful house, a new car, a comfortable life that most others might envy.

But all through our marriage, I felt it. A tug that drew me away from the picture-perfect life I was leading and toward the one I really wanted. I tried to ignore it—and for years I succeeded. But if I were to really be honest with myself, I would have had to admit that I had felt it for as long as I could remember.

After a dozen years in my marriage, my decision became clear: I needed to leave. For years, I had let the current of what other people wanted me to be sweep me further and further away from the life I really wanted. I knew there was more to life than driving a nice car and trying out the hot new restaurant in town. There was a spiritual side as well, and it was calling to me. Finally, I listened.

After my divorce, things weren't easy: at one point, I even contemplated going on welfare. But through it all, I learned to have faith in myself. I learned to follow where my heart led me. And it led me, finally, to Angel's Gate.

That Christmas Eve, the ASPCA van pulled up in front of our house. A uniformed worker flung open the van's rear doors, and helped the dog out. A Great Dane mix, he was so malnourished he looked like a ghost: every rib bone stuck out like a stirrup. He had a huge head that teetered above a frail fifty-two-pound frame that should have been carrying at least twice that weight. The right side of his face was paralyzed, as if from a stroke—his eye drooped, his jaw was slack. Crip-

pling arthritis contorted him, making his outline look almost like a question mark. He traveled on his hocks, so that with each painful step it looked more like he was sitting than walking.

"He'll probably only be here a few weeks," I thought, as the van doors slammed shut and the big black figure took a few hesitant steps forward. "So

we'll make them the best few weeks
of his life."

The dog walked unsteadily toward
the house; given his physical condition, this seemed like a miracle in
itself. Actually what he did was more
like stumbling, and with his twisted posture, his haunches were
only an inch off the ground. Despite the pain he was clearly
suffering, he seemed almost curious about where he was going.
And though he had lost his center of gravity and teetered pre-
cariously, he never lost his composure. He seemed almost regal.

We held the door open, and he made his way into the hall.
Curious, he swung his massive head to the right, peering into
the formal living room that we use as an office. The green glow
of the computer screen, the stack of Angel's Gate pamphlets,
the snoozing cat on the copy machine—he took it all in.

By the time he returned his focus to the hall, a large knot
of our animals had crowded around to see him. There was
Betty, an independent hound mix who had mammary cancer,
and Schultze, a scrappy black-and-tan dachshund who had
lost all function in his rear legs. Dragging herself right behind
them was Sarah, the paralyzed Tibetan spaniel who had left
another puddle in her wake. And there was Katie, a black-and-
white three-legged cat who saunters through life, apparently
unaware that she's missing a limb.

With most new arrivals, my Angel's Gate welcoming committee would have rushed in, sniffing and poking and prodding. But there was something different about this one, and they felt it. Quietly, respectfully, they parted, and let him shuffle into the house.

Purposefully, he walked to the sliding doors next to the kitchen table and looked out into the inky dark backyard. Seemingly satisfied, he went a few more feet and then settled down between the wall and the kitchen table with a deliberateness that seemed to border on familiarity, as if he had lived here his whole life. When it became obvious he wouldn't budge, I got a few big soft blankets for him, and he resettled contentedly on them and drifted off to sleep.

I sat down in front of our still undecorated tree and flipped through the case file that had accompanied the dog. The paperwork was an inch thick—too much for me to read tonight. But one page caught my eye.

The ASPCA case worker had drawn a thick black line through the dog's old name, Timmy, and offered him a new identity to go with his new life.

"Lucky," she had scrawled. "Going to Angel's Gate."

Merry Christmas, Lucky, I thought, as I dimmed the kitchen lights and headed off to bed.

Humphrey

The next day, after the presents were opened and the dishes were washed and the company had left, I had a chance to go through Lucky's file more carefully.

Lucky had installed himself in the kitchen, and I knew that this was where he would spend his final days. All the animals that come to Angel's Gate find their own little niche somewhere in the house, a place from which to contemplate the world.

Vic had noticed Lucky's declaration of real estate as well, and had moved the kitchen table farther away from the wall so Lucky could maneuver more easily. The sliding doors to the backyard were only a few feet away; periodically he stood up and let us know he needed to relieve himself, another miracle, considering he had lived outside most of his life and had never been housebroken.

I sat down at the kitchen table with the fat ASPCA file, and Lucky acknowledged my presence with a long stare. His tail remained motionless. I admired his handsome head, which had tracings of white around the eyes and muzzle. He reminded me of a decorous old gentleman, the kind you see in eternal contemplation on a park bench.

I flipped through the papers, noting the usual tests and procedures—x-rays of his battered head, blood panels and fecal cultures, eye washes, doses of the antibiotic Baytril for his infected ear, and Cosequin and Rimadyl for his arthritis. But one piece of paper seemed incongruous—a photocopy of an article about racehorse injuries. Thinking it had been misfiled, I set it aside and continued on through the pile of papers.

Over and over, the ASPCA vets used the same words to describe Lucky: "old," "geriatric," "debilitated." Through the shorthand and the rushed penmanship, which day after day repeated the same facts without much hope for improvement, I read between the lines for the conclusion: euthanasia. From a medical point of view, it was a logical recommendation. But at Angel's Gate, a diagnosis is not destiny. With Lucky, as with all our animals, we allowed for hope and serendipity, and the healing power of love. When Lucky was ready to die, he would. Until then, we would dote on him and care for him.

The case file also gave me glimpses of the gray existence Lucky had lived for more than a dozen years. Tied to a tree in a city backyard for most of his life, he had developed a chronic infection in his right ear that had permeated the bone in his ears, damaging the nerves and causing his right eye to sink in and the ear above it to droop. A neighbor, unable to watch the neglect anymore, eventually called animal control, and the dog was confiscated. The ear infections, I read, were a result of routine beatings, probably with a heavy object, such as a piece of lumber. Then I understood the reason for the equine article in the file: Lucky's injuries were typical of those sustained by racehorses that are routinely beaten about the head.

I heard a growl and looked up. Humphrey, a plucky Shih Tzu, had wandered over to inspect the new guest, but Lucky was not in the mood. He rumbled again, and the little black-and-white dog backed away, puzzled by this grumpy newcomer.

I knew Lucky was just being territorial: the ASPCA papers said that while he had a stable temperament with people, he was food-aggressive and wasn't particularly friendly with other dogs. I understood his reaction: he had finally found a soft, comfortable place, and he didn't want to share it.

But of all the animals to grumble at, Humphrey was an unfortunate choice. After all, if it wasn't for that little Shih Tzu, Lucky wouldn't have been here at all. When Lucky arrived on our doorstep that Christmas holiday in 1999, Angel's Gate was in full swing. After seven years of running the hospice, I had animals in every room, a network of volunteers and veterinarians, and an array of healing tools that ranged from canine wheelchairs to medicinal herbs.

But it wasn't always that way. In the beginning, there was just Humphrey.

♥ ♥ ♥

In 1992, I had just moved in with Vic, ready to start our life together. Caring for a tribe of critically ill and dying animals wasn't in our game plan. In fact, Vic had confided to me that after his elderly terrier mix Chelsea died, he didn't think he would get another animal: it was just too much responsibility.

One of our neighbors had the cutest Shih Tzu, with the breed's typically plucky personality. They came over distraught one day: Humphrey had a ruptured disc. They couldn't afford the $2,500 surgery, and the vet doubted that Humphrey would ever walk again anyway.

Over the years, I had become interested in holistic health care for both people and animals, and had attended seminars and lectures to expand my nursing knowledge to include everything from herbs to acupuncture. Humphrey's family had a word for it: "voodoo." But they were desperate: they didn't want to euthanize Humphrey, but they didn't feel they had any other choice. So they turned the paralyzed dog over to us.

The first thing Vic and I did was to take Humphrey to have

the much-needed back surgery. The doctors told us it was probably too late to see any results, and that Humphrey would be incontinent and immobile for the rest of his life.

But I didn't listen to that. After the surgery, I took Humphrey for regular acupuncture treatments, and I helped him swim every day in our heated pool. I also put him on a radical diet: a bona fide junk-food addict, Humphrey was profoundly obese. His family had dropped him off with the huge box of Milk-Bones that they dipped into every time he looked cute, which was often.

For six months, Humphrey went through a healing crisis. He oozed out of every orifice—he had constant diarrhea, and crud flowed from his eyes and ears—as all the toxins of a lifetime exited his body. We bought him a canine wheelchair so he could go wherever he wanted, and we worked with Humphrey for months, with seemingly no results. But it didn't matter—he was getting better, he was with us, and that was all we asked.

Then one day, Vic called to me urgently from the kitchen. I ran in, and there was Humphrey, standing wobbly at his water bowl. I was elated. Humphrey had worked so hard, and now it was paying off.

Within months, Humphrey was not only walking, he was scampering around the house like a puppy. Years passed, and he turned into a spunky and spry senior citizen who could get around without anyone's help. And though we didn't know it at the time, he was our first resident at Angel's Gate.

♥ ♥ ♥

Returning from my daydreaming and hearing another growl, I looked up again from the ASPCA file. In his good-natured way, Humphrey had tried another overture to Lucky, who still wasn't interested in being friends, or even acquaintances. If Humphrey could have shrugged, he would have. Instead, he trotted off to inspect the floor under the kitchen counter, hopeful that a morsel or two had fallen since he had last checked. Once a Milk-Bone junkie, always a Milk-Bone junkie.

Closing Lucky's thick file, I reached down to pat his bony, grimy head. He didn't react, but at least he accepted my touch. Earlier in the day, when Vic had knelt down to put a collar around his neck—with "Angel's Gate" and our phone number embroidered on it—he had reared back fearfully, wincing in anticipation of the pain to come.

I stroked his big head and murmured softly to him, and this time he looked up at me wearily. "I like it here fine so far," he seemed to be saying, as he stretched out on the blanket. "But I'm not sure I trust you quite yet."

It was clear: Lucky was making up his mind about us. The question was whether he would have enough time to come to a decision.

Radar

"Yuck!" Holding the end of the bulb syringe, I squeezed, and a glob of yellow-brown fluid landed in the container next to me. Still holding on tight to the rubber bulb, I put the tip back into Lucky's badly infected right ear, ready to extract still more gunk.

As I worked, Lucky lay like a statue on his blankets by the kitchen table. Every time I withdrew the syringe, his eyes followed its path, watching to see what I would do next. This dog, I had concluded, was an expert watcher. Nothing, no matter how minute, escaped his attention. He stared intently as I mopped the kitchen floor. He eyed me with interest as I sat down at the table to dropper-feed a baby pigeon that had been found barely alive in a busy intersection. Outside the sliding doors, the yard was covered in a quilt of snow, but he pressed his nose to the glass and inspected the delicate scrimshaw of tracks left by the sparrows.

After I was done with the syringe, I swabbed his ear with tea tree, an essential oil that soothed the inflamed tissue. Lucky grunted with pleasure.

I was amazed that he could even accomplish that small effort. Lucky had been at Angel's Gate for a month already, with barely any improvement. He was still thin and weak and old and, frankly, he was dying. Every week I took him to the veterinarian for acupuncture treatments for his severe arthritis, and at each visit the vet looked at me searchingly, wondering how Lucky had survived another week, and why I was investing all this time and money in a dog who was so close to death.

Still, I wasn't giving up hope. When I was a nurse, I often found that laughter, or just a simple expression of love, could be more healing than drugs. I believe healing comes from enthusiasm—enthusiasm means "God within" in Greek. That was a lesson I had learned from another dog—one I came to call Radar.

After our success with Humphrey in 1992, I had started lecturing at local kennel clubs, dog and cat groups, bird societies, library groups—anyone who would have me—about the incredible lessons we had learned from him. That just because an animal is paralyzed or incontinent doesn't mean he should be thrown away. That there are ways to cope with these challenges and still keep the company of the animal you love.

But instead of inspiring other people to care for their special-needs animals, it seemed I had prompted a flow of animals that people wanted to get rid of. And so these animals joined our household, along with Humphrey. In the beginning, I didn't call what I was doing hospice. It was just what I was doing.

♥ ♥ ♥

Soon after I started lecturing, a local vet asked me to come see a six-month-old Yorkie puppy who had been brought in as an emergency. He was lethargic and had difficulty breathing; in less than an hour, he was comatose.

When he finally came out of the coma two weeks later, the little dog was blind and deaf, and he spun in circles constantly, wearing the pads off his feet and splattering the sides of his cage with blood.

The stainless steel cage was cold and hard, so I held him in my lap. I got the sense that he was very disjointed, that he had no idea of his own body. So I started administering TTouch, a system of healing touches that helps the body reorient itself and opens neural pathways. After twenty minutes, I put him back on the floor, and he walked in a straight line.

"How did you do that?" everyone asked in amazement.

"I didn't do it," I said. "He did."

The little Yorkie's name was Spinner, and since to some extent I believe our names define us, that was the first thing we changed. I renamed Spinner Radar because, although he was totally blind, he never ran into anything.

In addition to his blindness, Radar was incontinent and deaf. We took him home, and we loved him into health. We used flower essences and essential oils, especially Heliochrysm, which helps restore nerve function. Radar got some of his hearing back—not a lot, but some. I'd hold him every night and sing "Jesus Loves Me," a hymn that my grandmother had sung to me when I was a little girl.

Now, sitting on the floor with Lucky, I debated whether he too would be receptive to a little cuddling. I leaned forward, and he looked at my hand intently, expecting the syringe or the cotton balls to reappear. But when the hand was empty, his eyes grew wide with suspicion and concern.

I started rubbing behind his ears, but he stiffened with each stroke. I could see that no matter how well-intentioned it was, my touch was causing him discomfort. So I hoisted myself up off the kitchen floor, and returned to my memories of Radar.

Despite his severe disabilities, the part of Radar that could love and be loved was very much alive. Whenever I held him, I felt positively lighthearted. People said Radar had nothing to give, but I knew how special I was to him. I felt unconditionally loved, and I loved him unconditionally.

I felt so at peace when I held Radar—after a hectic twelve-hour nursing shift, all I needed to do was hold him, and I was back in balance.

Then Radar began to have seizures and we discovered he had a liver shunt, a congenital malformation of the blood supply to the liver. He slept in a bassinet in our bedroom, draped with an oxygen tent. I didn't want to leave the house to go to work—I just wanted to stay home and care for him.

And so I did: I quit my job. I felt my job was at home, with the thirty animals we had by then brought into our house and our lives. Radar was the one who cemented that decision for me. In 1995, I left nursing forever, and veered off onto an entirely new path.

We tried surgery to repair the shunt, but right afterward Radar had a grand mal seizure. He was declining, and he started to lose weight.

Six months later, Radar died very quietly in my arms. In the end, he still walked in circles—but his circles had gotten bigger, and so had mine. After Radar passed, Angel's Gate opened its door to still more animals, and our circle of love widened.

♥   ♥   ♥

This is what I wanted for Lucky, I thought as I ran the hot water in the kitchen sink. I want bigger circles for him. It wasn't enough for him to get better and live out his final days in comfort. He needed to learn to love, and I knew that would sustain him, as it had Radar.

The tap water grew too hot, and I quickly pushed the cold-water lever to keep the rush from the faucet from scalding me. Maybe my expectations needed tempering too. Lucky and Radar were entirely different dogs, I reminded myself as I rinsed the soapy syringe and set it on the counter to dry. Radar had known nothing but love in his life. He had been held and kissed and coddled from cradle to grave. He had been given love, so he was able to return it in kind.

But what could I ask from Lucky? His whole life had been tethering and confinement, with days melting into weeks and years. At best, what he knew from his contact with people was neglect; at worst, he learned that human hands brought pain and mistreatment. His spirit had been wrung out like a dishrag, and at some point he had ceased to care.

But had he really? I could see how increasingly interested he was with the goings-on around him—he had even stood up when Vic came in with the groceries one day. And of all the rooms in the house, he had selected the busiest and most trafficked one to be in—if he had wanted a more solitary space, he could have retreated to the great room, where all that would disturb him was the occasional screech of a cockatoo. And he had allowed me to tend to him, stoic and proud, on his bed.

I looked down at the big black dog, and our eyes met. And while it might have just been the glint of sun reflecting off the January snow, I could swear I saw it: a glimmer of life in those weary black eyes.

Elmo

Struggling to close the sliding doors against a blast of February wind, Vic stomped the snow from his boots, depositing little piles of powder on the tile floor of the kitchen.

"I have a nickname for him," Vic said, unzipping his parka. "The Don."

"What?" I said, looking up from the jumble of bills, grant applications, and veterinary brochures on the kitchen table.

Vic has been my partner in life as well as in Angel's Gate, and the concept of opposites attracting has no better example than the two of us. Vic is a pragmatist who rolls his eyes at my talk of the importance of energies, the world of spirit, and the power of intention. Vic believes in what he can see and hear and touch. I believe that our animals are part of a larger plan, that they come into our lives for a reason, and that when their work is done, they depart physically, although they stay on in spirit. Vic believes that they are here just because they happen to be here, and when they go, they are gone for good.

Where I see a planet weaving a web of interconnectedness and divine purpose, Vic sees a swirl of chaos and coincidence. I believe in the continuity of what came before us and what comes after us; Vic acknowledges only the temporal bookends that we call our lives.

Yet he believes in the importance of the work that we are doing just as strongly as I do—and that every life, no matter how fragile, is precious.

"What do you mean, the Don?" I asked, looking at him from over my glasses. On the floor beside me, Lucky grumbled his annoyance at the chill Vic had let into the room, then burrowed his face deeper into the fleece bedding.

"He's like this Mafia boss, sitting there on his blankets," said Vic, settling into the chair next to me to remove his sodden boots. "Like Don Corleone holding court."

I hadn't thought about it in those terms, but Vic had a point. Without uttering a sound, without moving a muscle, Lucky commanded respect. People who visited the house invariably walked over to greet him. And they never patted his head roughly or slapped him on the back. They murmured respectfully, and they lowered their heads toward him. It wasn't quite kissing his ring, but it was close.

I think the reason Lucky elicited such deference was his energy. He was an old soul, and just looking at him, you knew he had a kind of wisdom that some creatures never gain, no matter how long their years. And his energy was all male— powerful yet protective, courageous yet contemplative.

♥ ♥ ♥

If there was an equine version of Lucky at Angel's Gate, it would be Elmo the pony, who lives with his longtime friend and partner Sarah in our backyard. That was where Vic had been this morning, using the snowblower to make a trail for the ponies in the freshly fallen snow, then strewing it with hay so they wouldn't slip and fall when it turned to ice.

In all honesty, I had never envisioned horses at Angel's Gate. But then again, if I had limited my life to what was in my imagination, Angel's Gate would be short of a lot of little miracles.

Elmo and Sarah's arrival was unexpected, to say the least. A friend who was a member of a horse association had mentioned that her stable needed some barn cats. Eager to give some strays a new lease on life, I stopped at the municipal shelter and picked a few who looked like they might be good mousers. But on the day I was supposed to drop them off, the barn manager called.

"I have to ask you not to come today," she said. "We're euthanizing a couple of ponies and we won't have time."

"What's wrong with the ponies?" I asked.

"Nothing, really," she replied. "They're just old."

For almost three decades, Elmo and Sarah had given rides to children at a day camp, always dependable in their gentleness and obedience. Then the day came that even the weight of a toddler was too much for them to bear. The ponies had outlived their usefulness.

"I'll take them," I said, the words flying out of my mouth.

I got off the phone, and faced my big hurdle: telling Vic. He had placed a moratorium—one of many—on my bringing home any more animals.

I'd learned by then that spin is everything. "I have such great news," I told him. "We're getting two ponies!"

"Susan, are you nuts?" he replied. "Do you know anything about ponies?"

"No," I answered honestly, "but I figure I'll learn whatever I need to know."

As soon as Elmo and Sarah arrived, Vic's heart softened, as I knew it would. We penned in a portion of the side yard for them, and Vic built a lean-to where they could eat and find shelter from the elements. I said a silent prayer of thanks that we had had the foresight to buy a piece of property that was zoned for farm use: we were allowed to have as many animals as we liked on our suburban acre-and-a-third. And now we had two ponies.

With the arrival of the ponies, the energy of Angel's Gate changed completely. I was still working full-time, and after I came home, totally exhausted, I'd go out to their corral and bury my face in Elmo's mane. There was something so energizing and simultaneously so relaxing about doing that. Then I'd just sit there for a while and watch them. They seemed so balanced, their lives so basic and simple. They lived to eat, they walked the property, and just seemed to love their lives.

In many ways, Lucky reminded me of Elmo. Both were clearly masculine spirits—tough, resilient, stoic, and passionate. Yet they were both gentle too. At thirty-three, Elmo was the kindly patriarch of Angel's Gate. All our rehabilitating ducks and geese are kept in  the pony pen, and no one's ever been injured there. It's Elmo's own little peaceable kingdom, and I'm comforted to know that he's watching over everything.

Elmo made me think a lot about purpose. Humans like to have careers, plans, directions. Everyone needs to have a function. If you don't—if you are taking time to figure out just what it is that you want to "do," or if what you do isn't concrete or valued by others—then by some measures you are considered worthless.

In Elmo's case, his worth had been measured by how many

children he could carry, and for how long. Period. And in his way, Elmo let us know that he didn't want to be defined by something as limiting as his age. After he and Sarah had been with us for a few years, we acquired Kandy Kisses, a forty-three-year-old palomino. Her name was an omen: when she walked into the corral, Elmo was smitten. Fortunately, Sarah wasn't jealous at all. Like a cynical older sister, she looked on, amused, as Elmo tried all sorts of ways to court Kandy. The problem was, Kandy was several hands taller than Elmo and, despite his ardor, he just couldn't make the anatomy work, though, God knows, he tried. Sarah just stood there watching, as if to say, "Are you out of your mind?"

"No," Elmo seemed to want to reply. "But I'm alive!"

To most people, old Lucky didn't have any more purpose than Elmo. He wasn't a show dog. He didn't do competitive obedience or agility. He wasn't a therapy dog, or a search-and-rescue dog, or a service dog. He was just a beloved dog. And at Angel's Gate, that was Lucky's job—to soak in as much love as he possibly could in the short time he had left.

"How is being loved a job?" people ask me.

"How is it not?" I answer.

Now, outside, I could see snow swirling across the barren backyard. Through the curtain of crystals over the glass doors I glimpsed Elmo, his head slung over the fence, eyeing the sea of white, his benign presence ensuring that all was in order.

Phoenix

Every household has its rhythms. Some are busier than others, with kids bursting through the back door for a snack, or neighbors popping over to borrow a tool or some vital ingredient for a recipe.

If I had to describe the rhythm at Angel's Gate, I would say it has a reggae beat. Infectious, insistent. And constant, without a break in the tempo.

Often, it seems as if our front door never closes. People visit our web site, jot down the address and drive over unannounced, overjoyed to see what we are doing, and asking for a tour.

To be honest, sometimes I'm feeling cranky or crazed, with too many animals to tend to and not much time for small talk.

But I always open the door wide and let visitors in, introduce them to the animals, answer questions about where we sleep (in the master bedroom, usually with a dozen dogs and cats joining us) or how we survive (on donations, which always seem to arrive just in time). Each person focuses on a different animal, asking why that cat walks funny or what that lump is on that dog's side.

But once Lucky arrived, everyone noticed him. They would walk into my kitchen and gape at his still-gaunt frame and his distorted head. I knew what they were thinking: that dog is dying.

And, by mid-February, seven weeks after his arrival, with no real improvement in this big, black, mysterious shell of a dog, I was beginning to agree. I had tried everything in my holistic repertoire—herbs, acupuncture, essential oils, homeopathy, a raw-food diet—but nothing was working.

Occasionally, veterinarians will visit Angel's Gate and inquire about the medical treatment the animals get. Often, if they are conventionally trained, with no room in their minds or spirits for alternative ways to heal, they leave angry or upset. They can't understand why I won't vaccinate any of my animals, even after I point out that the vaccine label itself says "not for use on sick animals"—and the animals at Angel's Gate are nothing if not sick. These vets reject the idea of feeding animals a biologically appropriate diet of raw meat and ground veggies.

In the beginning, I used to debate with skeptical vets, trying to get them to see the results I was getting. But then I realized that those who wanted to learn would, and the rest would not consider what I was saying, no matter how persuasive I was. Only when the student is ready does the teacher arrive.

Some of my most important teachers have been animals; in fact, I believe every animal at Angel's Gate is here to help me learn a lesson. Creating Angel's Gate was a process of trial and error, and as I began to take the animals into my home, I had plenty of moments of self-doubt and insecurity. I was unsure of myself and this holistic path I had taken.

Then along came Lady.

I have always had a soft spot for Afghan hounds. Maybe it's their majestic bearing, or their regal attitude. It seems I am never without one of those graceful, long-haired hounds, and Lady was my first.

I found her in 1994, through a newspaper ad that some home-based rescuers had placed. Their house was more like a horse stall than a shelter; Lady, an eight-month-old purebred Afghan puppy, was living in one of a dozen crates stacked against their bedroom wall. From inside the plastic dens, dogs of all sizes and shapes barked at me—a waggy-tailed shepherd mix, a wild-eyed Dalmatian. Lady just sat there, elegant and composed, watching me as if to say, "What in heaven's name took you so long?"

Yes, I told the couple, I would love to take her, and they removed her from the cramped crate. Even though Afghan hounds are supposed to be lithe and graceful, with protruding hip bones that are a hallmark of the breed, Lady looked especially skinny.

"She's just getting over kennel cough," the woman said, handing me a bottle of antibiotics. "This will clear it up."

But I soon discovered that Lady didn't have kennel cough. She had something much more serious—distemper. The local vet made a house call to give me the diagnosis, prescribed more antibiotics, and suggested that she be hospitalized.

I decided to keep her home instead. This tattered aristocrat of a puppy had been through enough, I felt, and I knew that treating her in a familiar setting would be best. I also had a gut feeling that conventional medicine was not the way to treat the disease that had taken hold of Lady. My instinct was to try some of the nontraditional healing approaches I had begun to study, but had never put into use—at least never in a situation that was do-or-die.

Homeopathy. The word popped into my head, but I resisted it. After all, I didn't know very much about this holistic modality, which is much more accepted in Europe than it is in this country. I was at a crossroads: should I give Lady the antibiotics the conventional vet had prescribed, or should I seek out a homeopathic vet and do what my instinct told me?

Doubtful and distressed, I struggled with the question for hours. The more I agonized, the more I felt the fear. Fear of failing, fear of contradicting the norm, fear of the unknown. In the end, I decided, the only thing that was more powerful than the uncertainty I was experiencing was pure, simple faith.

I had no more excuses left: I had to trust my instincts, even if my plan sounded completely nuts, which it did to just about everybody, including my vet and even Vic. Determined, I locked myself in the basement with Lady, isolating us so that the infectious disease could not travel to the other animals in the house. I slept by her side as she fasted, giving her water and honey in an attempt to keep her hydrated.

I found a homeopathic vet in New Mexico who consulted with me over the phone, prescribing various remedies that Vic would get from the health-food store, then leave for me outside the basement door. I could hear the footsteps of Vic and Dantae above me, as they burned dinners and carted out bags of dirty clothes to the laundromat.

Meanwhile, Lady worsened. Thick green mucus oozed from her nose, and her temperature soared, reaching a hellish 106 degrees. Relying on my thirty years of nursing experience, I kept her hydrated with intravenous fluids, and set up an oxygen tent to help with her labored breathing.

Despite twice-a-day consults with the homeopathic vet, Lady grew even weaker. When she had lost half her body weight, the conventional vet suggested euthanasia. I held Lady in my arms, and cried myself to sleep. She was dying, and I felt I had failed her.

Now, years later, I look back at my experience with Lady and realize how much I have grown since. I no longer think about each animal's fate as a failure or a success, because it's not about me anymore. I do my best for my animals, and then I step back and let nature take its course.

I woke the next morning from the basement vigil with Lady to find her licking my face, exhausted and hungry. She felt cool, and her fever was gone. As suddenly as it had descended on her, the distemper had receded. She was weak and thin, but she was alive. I had listened to my instincts, and she had survived.

Three weeks after that very sick Afghan puppy and I went underground, literally, we reemerged from the basement triumphant. Lady had survived the distemper that everyone said would kill her, and she had an appropriate new name—Phoenix. And I had gotten over my self-doubt, and had replaced it with a new awe for the healing methods I had used, and a new trust in following my instincts.

♥ ♥ ♥

As for Lucky, all I could think about was making him more comfortable during his final days. So I turned my attention to his bed: actually, it wasn't a bed at all, just a pile of blankets, because he was too big for anything else.

If Lucky didn't fit on a conventional dog bed, we would give him a human one, I decided. So Vic rooted around in the basement, brought up an old waterbed frame, and fitted it with a thick foam mattress.

And that was what did it. Not an herb or a special homeopathic remedy. Not a cocktail of vitamins and enzymes, or a miracle drug. What made Lucky decide to live, as incredible as it sounds, was that bed. From the minute we put him on it, he began to improve. It was as if he had thought all along that he was accidentally on the wrong side of the kitchen's sliding glass doors, that one day he would be put back outside, cold and lonely. But once that shapeless pile of blankets was replaced with a real, honest-to-goodness bed, he believed in his good luck.

As visitors glimpsed him on his new bed, they were still overcome by Lucky's frailty, and most thought that the first time they met him would turn out to be the last. But I could clearly see improvement, though it was gradual and relative. Now that Lucky had decided to believe in us—that his new life was *not* too good to be true—his body responded to his treatments. The herbs and essential oils soothed the damaged tissues in his ear; the natural diet began to clear his system.

Yes, he was painfully thin, and you could still count his ribs, but now they didn't stick out. Yes, his head was still sunken in and the ear infection lingered, but at least now he could hold his head up for longer than a few seconds. That was progress—painfully slow progress, but progress.

And as his body repaired itself and his pain ebbed a bit, I knew that Lucky could heal an even bigger part of himself—his spirit.

Schultze

I don't want to make it sound like Lucky was a saint, because he wasn't. He was a cranky old man by the time we got him. I would have loved to have known him in his heyday. There was just something appealing about him—there was a twinkle in his eye.

And he was tough. He had to be to survive what he had. He was rough around the edges, a little gruff. But when you would sit with him and he'd lay his head in your lap, you'd touch him, and he'd just melt. Some tough guy!

However, Lucky's soft spot didn't extend to any of the other animals in the house. Acknowledging his rumbles and growls, they had all learned to steer clear of his beloved bed—

all except for one persistent little dog, a crusty black-and-tan dachshund named Schultze.

A degenerative disc problem had left Schultze paralyzed, and he came to Angel's Gate when his family decided they couldn't deal with his incontinence and his bedsores. From the very first day Lucky arrived, Schultze would drag himself over to the big dog's bed to inspect his sleeping quarters. Lucky eyed him warily.

They were a study in contrasts—the leggy, oversized Great Dane mix and the stubby little dachsie. Tied to a tree all his life, Lucky had never had a friend, had never made a connection more fleeting than the sad glances he got from neighbors as they came out to their adjoining yards to water their vegetable gardens or hang laundry.

Now Schultze had decided to become Lucky's friend—a decision that Lucky didn't appreciate. He'd look disdainfully

at the little dog, and growl and bark. And, with his determined dachshund personality, Schultze would bark right back, smugly realizing that the big black dog couldn't reach him even if he tried. Then Lucky would lower his head in disgust and close his eyes.

There's no logical reason why Schultze was so drawn to a dog that was twenty times his size. Or why Lucky came to tolerate him, no matter how grudgingly. Sometimes friendship is like that—unexplainable, and magical.

♥ ♥ ♥

I can tell when two animals have that bond, and then I know I need to keep them together at all costs. Gimbel and Junie were a perfect example.

Gimbel was a kitty cover girl—a beautiful silver-tipped Persian, with a long, flowing coat that you just had to touch and stroke. Junie was a big gal, a tabby who looked like your run-of-the-mill street cat. Despite their physical differences, Gimbel and Junie were sisters under the skin, and they shared a special bond.

Raised together since kittenhood, Gimbel and Junie were sent to a shelter after the elderly woman who had raised them died. There, Gimbel was diagnosed with lymphoma, and given only weeks to live. The shelter's plan was to euthanize Gimbel, and find Junie a new home. But the woman's dying wish had been that they not be separated. My friend Lucille, who did cat rescue, learned about Gimbel and Junie, and brought both of them to Angel's Gate.

I was determined to make Gimbel's last days as pleasurable as possible, and we waited on her hand and foot: we rubbed her ears, we stroked her gorgeous coat, we offered her delicious meals that she gobbled up readily.

Then, suddenly, she was dead. Not Gimbel—her healthy sister, Junie!

I couldn't believe it: suddenly Junie, who had been perfectly fine, was dead, and Gimbel, who should have been barely alive, was looking and acting normal. So I took Gimbel to the vet to find out how much time the beautiful Persian had left.

"This cat doesn't have lymphoma," the vet said. "She has very small kidneys, which is why they may have misdiagnosed her. But she's as healthy as any cat I've seen today."

On the ride home, I thought about Gimbel's misdiagnosis. If I had believed the shelter and let them euthanize her, both cats would have been dead within a week—Junie from an illness that we never did diagnose, and Gimbel from a medical error.

Instead, by honoring their relationship, and the dying wish of the woman who had loved them, I had given Gimbel a new lease on life, and Junie the dignity of a peaceful death, with her sister nearby. I wondered if Junie had hung on for so long to make sure Gimbel ended up okay. When we allow them to follow their own internal timetables, I believe animals always choose to leave at just the right time.

♥ ♥ ♥

Sometimes the animals at Angel's Gate bond with each other; other times, it's one special human that they are inexplicably drawn toward, like Lizzie was to Dantae.

A perky Yorkshire terrier, all long hair and attitude, Lizzie lived with an autistic child. One day, he picked her up and tried to snap her in half. He almost succeeded, and Lizzie came to us paralyzed.

With hydrotherapy, herbs, and acupuncture, Lizzie learned to walk again. Now she runs and plays almost as well as she used to, except for a little hitch in her gait. She became very attached to my daughter Dantae, following her wherever she went, sleeping in her arms at night.

My youngest daughter has always taken the lessons she's learned at home out into the world with her. At age five, she started writing eulogies for all the animals that died at Angel's Gate. As a grade-schooler, she refused to dissect frogs in biology class, and she has gotten very involved in animals-rights campaigns, even flying down to Florida to help circulate petitions protesting everything from force-feeding ducks to make foie gras to using the urine of pregnant mares to relieve women's menopause symptoms.

Now, at sixteen, she is struggling with that all-consuming teenage obsession—becoming her own self. She knows she wants to spend her life helping animals, but she doesn't think it will be in the same way I do. And that's fine with me. When I watch Dantae hug Lizzie close to her, I know that the lessons and values she learned living at Angel's Gate are planted deep inside her, waiting for their time to blossom.

♥ ♥ ♥

It was almost March when Schultze decided that enough was enough with the cranky big black dog. It was too cold to go outside for anything more than a quick pee, and pulling his paralyzed legs behind him through the lingering snow left him shivery. All the good cuddling spots in the house were taken— the once-white sofa in the office, all the dog beds in the family room, even the cushy quilt on my king-size bed.

Lucky's bed, warmed by the late afternoon sun, was just too inviting to pass up. So the plucky dachshund dragged himself purposefully to the foot of the bed, where he knew Lucky couldn't reach him, and plopped down with a thud.

Lucky lifted his head and looked at the black-and-tan gatecrasher, who was snuggled in the curve of his rear legs. A growl started up in his throat, then petered out, like a stalled engine. Annoyed but resigned to his fate, Lucky lowered his head on the mattress and closed his eyes in defeat. And on the far end of the mattress, Schultze sighed contentedly, snuggling closer to his reluctant new friend.

Tom-Tom

I waited patiently as the camerawoman fumbled with my jacket.

"I think that should do it," she said finally, standing back to see whether my microphone was secure.

It was one of my first television appearances, on a program hosted by a local veterinarian. He sat across from me on the studio set, studying his notes intently, occasionally adjusting his wire-rimmed glasses.

Next to me sat Vic. He straightened his tie and shifted in his chair, getting ready to share the limelight with me.

Center stage is not a place Vic finds himself all that often. I love to be out front, advocating and lecturing and spreading the message about Angel's Gate; he is much more likely to be behind the scenes, raking out the pony corral or patching the wire of the coops where we keep our convalescing geese and seagulls. Because of my emergency-room training, I thrive on fluidity and change, and am at my best in a crisis. Vic is drawn to the steady, stabilizing, daily rhythms of the household, organizing the volunteers, and providing patient, consistent care to some of our most demanding residents.

Like Chester, for instance. This 230-pound paraplegic mastiff was incontinent and needed to be bathed every day, then strapped into his canine cart. Vic did that heavy lifting, day in and day out. When Chester eventually died from stomach cancer, I'm sure Vic was relieved that this huge physical burden was lifted from him. But there was also incredible sadness that a dog he had invested so much in was gone forever.

When I first met Vic, I was worried that he wouldn't be able to embrace my love of animals. And there was no turning point, no "aha!" moment, when he was converted to the idea of devoting our lives to caring for a house full of animals. It was just a mild transition, a gradual, gentle acceptance. Slowly, our household grew, and our mission with it.

I have a memory of Vic that sums up how nurturing he is in his quiet, unassuming way. We had just taken in Spanky, an eight-month-old pit bull puppy with a deformed foot—his paw was literally split in two. An orthopedic vet had reconstructed the paw, and we were rehabbing Spanky for a rescue group that would later place him for adoption. But first he needed to heal—and that meant staying off his feet.

I was walking past the office where Vic was doing some paperwork and I heard his voice, calming and earnest. "Now, Spanky," he said, pulling the wriggling puppy into his lap, "you really need to calm down." When I came by a half-hour later, I peered in to see Spanky sprawled on Vic's lap, the two of them snoozing contentedly by the glow of the computer screen.

Of course, Vic still issues moratoriums on the number of animals we can take in, and I still ignore them. He complains all the time about the animals being in our bed, and I can see his point: if you're the last one to turn in, it can be tough to get a piece of real estate on our king-sized expanse.

But for all his griping, Vic is just as committed as I am to Angel's Gate. What attracted me most to him when we first met was that I found I could be whoever I was, and he was fine with it. No matter what decisions I make, he's always there to support me. When I told him my vision of our home as a residence for dying and disabled animals, his reaction wasn't "Are you nuts?" It was "What do you need to accomplish that?"

At Angel's Gate, Vic lets me run the show, but the show wouldn't go on without him. So when Vic was invited to join me on television and he agreed, I was thrilled.

While Vic was an impromptu addition to the taping, I had carefully selected the four animals that accompanied us on the set, because each represented a certain facet of Angel's Gate and our philosophy. There was Humphrey, the once-paralyzed Shih Tzu, who illustrated the importance of never giving up hope. Radar, the deaf and blind Yorkie, sat in my lap, his frailty and utter helplessness emphasizing the sanctity of all life, no matter how severe the disability. We brought a blind cat named Amazing Grace who, with her twitchy-tailed curiosity, showed how we cannot merely face our limitations, but transcend them. And, of course, how could we not take Lucky, who required everything that we believe hospice should provide—not just physical care, but all the love and dignity he had been robbed of?

When we walked onto the set, the vet's eyes scanned Lucky, and he did a double take. "He looks awfully thin," he said. I wasn't sure what he was really trying to say: that we didn't feed him enough? That viewers would tune out because he wasn't easy to look at?

"Here's a picture of what Lucky looked like when he came to us," I said, handing a photo to him.

He looked down at the haunted, gaunt image of Lucky twenty pounds lighter, and his eyes widened. Then, wordlessly, he returned to his notes.

♥ ♥ ♥

Long after that show was taped, a cat named Tom-Tom arrived at Angel's Gate. I would have loved to have brought him with us to the show. He made Lucky look like Jack La Lanne!

To describe Tom-Tom as a feline pretzel wouldn't be hyperbole. A year earlier, he had been hit by a car, and had dragged himself home with severe orthopedic injuries. The woman he lived with was a cat collector—someone who compulsively acquires animals even though she does not have the means or the facilities to care for them. According to her, the vet said that Tom-Tom's back was broken and that he had no feeling in his body. And so she never took him back to the vet.

But Tom-Tom could feel pain all right. And eventually, after months of physical torment, he did heal. But with no casts or surgeries to guide his broken body, he mended into a living corkscrew.

Both of Tom-Tom's rear legs had been fractured, and now, completely paralyzed, they jutted out from his body like weird antennae. One stuck straight forward, almost parallel to his spine, so that his toes grazed his chin. The other bent backward, following behind him like a furry rudder. Tom-Tom's tail, also broken in the accident, shot straight up in the air, like a flagpole. It hurt just to look at him.

When Tom-Tom arrived at Angel's Gate, dropped off by a rescue group that had been called to the collector's home, we were afraid to even touch him, much less pick him up. And he desperately needed handling: his fur and skin were caked with feces, and his nails were so overgrown they curled over and punctured the pads of his feet.

"Hello, there," I said reaching out gingerly to give him a gentle rub on the head, one of the few parts of his body that wasn't grossly deformed.

Impatiently, Tom-Tom pushed hard into my outstretched hand, guiding it further along his broken body. And then he began to purr.

It turned out that all Tom-Tom wanted was to be touched. In fact, he didn't just *want* human contact with his twisted, contorted self, he craved it.

Tom-Tom taught us, step by step, how to be with a handicapped cat. He didn't have time for pity, and always saw the glass as half full. Since Tom-Tom's lifeless rear legs got in his way when he walked, he chose instead to focus on the two that did work: he walked in a handstand, lifting his back end high in the air to keep it out of his way.

Tom-Tom's one concession to his handicap was wearing a diaper. His oddly angled limbs, extending from him like an octopus with petrified tentacles, made it impossible for him to use the litterbox; he invariably would get lodged in there. The diapers gave him his freedom, and so he accepted them readily. But other than that, he was just a regular cat whose legs just happened to go off in weird ways.

♥ ♥ ♥

As the camera crew dashed to their positions and the producer started the countdown to filming, I hoped that's what the audience would see: loveable, wonderful animals who just happened to be paralyzed or old or handicapped. And as Vic and I talked about the work we did at Angel's Gate, my animal quartet proved our point silently but eloquently. Radar sat calmly in my lap as I stroked him. On the floor, Humphrey settled down with a contented sigh at the vet's feet, his head on his front paws and his rear legs still strapped into his canine cart. Curious and confident, Amazing Grace explored the studio, returning to the set periodically to weave through our legs or rub up against the chairs.

And at the center of this television tableau, as at the center of our lives, was Lucky. Vic held his leash, but that was just a formality—Lucky wasn't going anywhere. He sat politely for the entire half-hour taping, looking off into the distance, but listening intently to every word.

Zeta

The program aired on a Saturday morning, and by noon the phone was ringing off the hook with people who wanted to know more about what we did, or how to make a donation, or whether they could sign up to volunteer.

These days, even more than money, people's most precious commodity is their time. And sometimes I think that many eager volunteers expect that the handful of hours they spend at Angel's Gate will be like a Disney movie—filled with doe-eyed, cartoon-cute creatures who are constantly entertaining and brimming over with mystical wisdom. That's not to say that Angel's Gate doesn't have its magical moments, or very special animals who amaze us with their intuitiveness and insight. But the daily grind of running a hospice isn't exactly a romantic vision. There's an awful lot of mundane repetition and monotonous tasks, from endless loads of laundry to countless passes of the mop.

So when a voice on the other end of the line said her name was Ann and she had felt inexplicably drawn to the big black dog on the television screen, I invited her to attend our volunteer orientation a few days later, but I didn't assume she'd become a regular. After all, seeing Lucky on TV was one thing; caring for him day to day was another. And if, after a few visits with a stiff old dog whose chronically infected ear, despite all our ministrations, still smelled like something had crawled into it and died, she decided never to come back, I would certainly understand. This work isn't for everyone, and many of our volunteers reluctantly come to that conclusion after a few visits.

But Ann wasn't put off by meeting Lucky in person. In fact, the more she visited, the more she wanted to do for him. Barely four months after Lucky came to Angel's Gate, Easter season, that celebration of rebirth, had arrived. Ann decided that instead of giving something *up* for Lent, she wanted to take something *on*. And she wanted that something to be Lucky.

Initially, Lucky was underwhelmed. To him, the petite fifty-something divorcee who stroked his head and crooned to him was just another nice person passing through. And in the beginning, there was his habitual hesitation to trust a new person. The longer Lucky stayed at Angel's Gate, the fainter his mistrust of people grew, but a piece of it was always with him.

But Ann persisted. She brought Lucky specially cooked meals, and talked to him gently and constantly as she scrubbed the kitchen floor, the counters, everything within eyeshot of his bed. Ann had decided that the place where Lucky slept, and the immediate vicinity, needed to be immaculate. We always joked that we knew when Ann had come over to volunteer because Lucky's freshly laundered bed linens were always color coordinated.

In her persistent determination to make Lucky love and trust her, Ann was very much like Schultze. And like Schultze, she eventually succeeded. When Ann walked in the door, I could see a change in Lucky. He would light up, as if Grandma had come to visit: here was his chance to be spoiled and doted on. Sure, he felt special being at Angel's Gate, but, like harried parents, Vic and I were often busy making sure the essentials were met, and that all of our animals were fed and cared for. Ann loved Lucky the way a grandparent loves—singularly, blindly, indulgently.

If I could have one wish for the animals in my hospice, it would be that each one would have an Ann of his or her own. Just one person who could take them to a quiet corner of the house and dote on them—just them—who would snuggle with them, and let them know they are the most special animals on earth.

In her weekly visits, Ann did that for Lucky. And another volunteer named Denise did it for a special little cat named Zeta.

♥ ♥ ♥

Denise was a volunteer who had read about Angel's Gate in a *People* magazine article, and immediately signed on as a volunteer. When she came over, she told me she was pleasantly surprised: she didn't think our hospice would be in an actual house, and she found the energy peaceful, and not at all depressing.

A few months after Denise arrived, so did Zeta. At the time, Zeta didn't have a name, only a diagnosis: cerebellar hypoplasia. Contracted in utero from her mother, who had distemper, the neurological disorder impeded her coordination, making her head rock and wracking her movements with spasms.

Denise fell in love with the wobbly one-year-old cat on the spot. Zeta was so friendly, so affectionate, running to the door as soon as someone new came in, even if she fell four times in the process. Unlike most of her species, this cat also accepted baths readily—all she wanted to do was please. When she saw Denise, she would rush to her, even if it meant walking around hazards like Chester the mastiff, who would growl at her for daring to invade his space. But Zeta didn't care—all she wanted was to get to Denise as quickly as possible.

Denise had searched for a name that reflected the beauty of this cat. Somehow, the actress Catherine Zeta-Jones came to her mind, and "Zeta" just seemed to fit.

Denise told me she would think about her visits with Zeta all week. And though she was a self-described "dog person," somehow this cat had claimed her heart. So when Denise walked in one day and said, "Where's my girl?" the words just tumbled out.

"Well," I replied, "do you want her?"

Denise burst into tears. She had wanted to ask me if she could take Zeta home, but she knew it was against the rules of the hospice to adopt animals out once they take up residence here.

That was true, I told her. But the relationship between her and Zeta was so strong that I knew that the best thing for Zeta would be to be with Denise. So I explained that while Angel's Gate was still primarily responsible for Zeta, and would continue to pay for her medical care, Denise could be her foster mother. I just needed to run some bloodwork to make sure that Zeta was as healthy as she looked, for aside from her wobbling, she was a normal young cat. And when the tests came back, they were perfect. Zeta was ready for her new home, and her very own person.

♥ ♥ ♥

Now, as I watched Ann fuss over Lucky, bathing and brushing him, I knew this was what he needed too: someone who would shine in his life.

Every week, Ann brought Lucky a huge marrow bone. As she unwrapped it, his tail thumped in anticipation. If any of the household's other dogs got a whiff of Lucky's prize and started to hover nearby, Ann would shoo them away before Lucky could even think about issuing his signature growl. Lucky could take a break when Ann was around!

Lucky had been dealt so many injustices in his long, abuse-filled life, and Ann wanted to make up for each and every one. Everything she did for him—every stroke of his head, every tug of the sweet-smelling linens on his newly made bed—conveyed that.

And as Lucky would take the bone between his huge paws, Ann would bend over and whisper in his ear. If you listened closely, you could hear what she was saying: Ann was apologizing for that life of pain.

"I'm sorry," she whispered as Lucky gnawed contentedly on his bone. "I am so very sorry."

Ann treated every day as if it was Lucky's last, and for good reason. Though he was doing incredibly well for a fifteen-year-old dog, he had already far surpassed the life expectancy of most dogs his size.

But there was no way we could have foreseen what would happen to Zeta. A few days before Denise planned to pick her up and take her to her home, the little cat suddenly grew ill. What happened to her is still a mystery. We didn't know what she had, but we knew that she didn't have much time to live.

We needed to contact Denise, but we didn't have her work number. Vic remembered that she worked for the county water authority, and he looked up the number. The phone rang and rang, and finally someone answered. There were more than three dozen people answering customer-service lines at the water authority that day. But when someone picked up the phone, that someone was Denise.

"Something's wrong with Zeta," Vic told her, and she could hear the gravity in his voice.

Denise got to Angel's Gate in what seemed like minutes, and not a moment too soon. A half hour after she arrived, Zeta died in her arms.

Amazing Grace

Could Lucky feel?

No one would dispute that on a physical level, our big black dog had registered all the pain of a lifetime spent being ignored and isolated—the limb-numbing cold of the New York City winters, the drumbeat-like throb of his infected ear and head, the fresh aches of the most recent beating from the person who had left him tied to a tree for years.

Now, at Angel's Gate, he knew all the good things that his sense of touch could deliver to him—the pleasure of a human hand stroking his flanks, the fleecy warmth of his favorite blanket, the soothing trickle of the tea tree oil I rubbed into his oozing ear.

Some animal behaviorists would say that a creature's consciousness basically stops there, like a truck slamming on the brakes in sudden traffic. Beyond those physical sensations and some basic emotions, such as fear, they argue, animals don't feel complex emotions the way humans define them. They would say that Lucky didn't know happiness, except perhaps as the absence of discomfort. Compassion and love, sadness and grief—all these emotions are outside the province of animals, these scientists say. Animals cannot laugh or mourn or pine any more than they are capable of writing a Dear John letter or chuckling at a funny movie. Anything else is just wishful thinking on our part.

But there are others who believe that animals don't only react out of instinct or hormonal drives. That they are thinking, feeling beings who have a capacity for humor, grief, and even love. I know Lucky felt all those emotions, and more. All I needed to do was watch him respond to his new home to know it was true.

As winter melted into spring, so did the wall that Lucky had created around himself. Schultze had taken a big chance when he crashed Lucky's bed, and it had paid off. The two were now inseparable, and there is no better word than love to describe the bond that grew between them, stronger every day.

Watching Lucky and Schultze was like watching reflections in a mirror—although, given the contrast of their physiques, funhouse mirror might be a more accurate image. When Lucky ate, Schultze came over to nibble, too, even if he wasn't hungry. When Schultze got up from the bed, Lucky dutifully tagged along. Neither was the leader nor the follower—they took turns guiding each other, and did everything in harmony. And if any other animal dared to approach their cozy bed, they would lift their heads in unison and growl.

As the buds on the trees swelled and the gauge on the outdoor thermometer cautiously crept upward, Lucky ventured outside, with Schultze dragging himself along at the bigger dog's heels. Haltingly, Lucky made the rounds of our backyard, discovering every inch. He surveyed the covered swimming pool. He inspected the tennis court. He paused in front of the corral and touched noses with Elmo the pony.

Lucky would have stayed outside for hours, inspecting his newfound kingdom, but we worried that the still nippy weather would sap him of his strength. Then one day, Ann arrived with presents—a teal-green sweater trimmed in white for Lucky, and a matching red one for his ever-present dachshund shadow.

That sweater was probably the first possession Lucky had ever had. Pride is an emotion we don't often associate with animals: somehow, we think it's the exclusive province of humans to be pleased with who and where we are in life, and to broadcast that dignity and sense of self-satisfaction to the world. But Lucky embodied it. And when Lucky wore that teal-green sweater to make his daily rounds, he radiated pride in every step.

♥ ♥ ♥

So did another elderly member of our household, the cat we called Amazing Grace. Grace was a rail-thin tabby—she weighed all of three pounds—who was totally blind. She had come from a shelter and, like many of our animals, we didn't know the details of her life, but we could tell it had been a hard one. Like Lucky, she was mistrustful, and the way she shied away from human hands told the story of what most of her experiences with people had been like.

When Grace had first arrived, we had called her Miss Daisy, for the dainty white "gloves" on each of her feet that reminded us of the proper southern lady in *Driving Miss Daisy.*

And like the Jessica Tandy character in that famous movie, our feline version was frail, geriatric, and strong-willed. But the similarities stopped there. The cinematic Miss Daisy was an inflexible curmudgeon, relying on others to help her navigate through life, emotionally as well as physically. Our Miss Daisy, on the other hand, didn't need anyone's help: when food was served, she shouldered her way into the pack and demanded her fair share, if not more. And despite her blindness, she could negotiate anywhere in the house, leaping onto a cat tree or chasing one of the dogs off the bed.

Soon after she arrived, Miss Daisy determined that the best

spot for her to sleep was on top of my head. Padding across the pillows, she'd burrow in, scratching and kneading my long brown hair until she had constructed a perfect nest for herself. It made turning over in my sleep a feat worthy of a circus contortionist, but Miss Daisy had made up her mind, and I wasn't likely to change it.

In fact, no one dared cross Miss Daisy. One day she marched into the kitchen while a dozen of our dogs milled around, awaiting lunch. All had lived at Angel's Gate long enough to know to steer clear of her—except for a young German short-haired pointer boarding with us while his family vacationed.

His eyes opened wide at the sight of Miss Daisy and, slowly, he approached her, until the two were nose to nose. Miss Daisy sniffed him impatiently.

Wildly, the pointer looked around, stunned that none of his canine brethren had noticed the cat in their midst. Then, calling on generations of hardwired hunting instincts, he did what any self-respecting sporting dog would do: he pointed. Feet rooted to the tile floor, paw flexed and steady as if carved from Carrara marble, he held that stance for minutes, practically vibrating with intensity, in the hopes *someone* would notice.

No one did, and that no one included Miss Daisy. Ignoring the statue-still pointer, the little blind cat marched through the throng, putting each foot down as confidently as the last, until she rounded the corner, tail swishing behind her.

As time went on, we decided that Miss Daisy was not the right name for this cat. While her movie namesake was nothing if not proud, her pride was a brittle and self-centered kind, based on how much money she had in the bank and what her neighbors thought of her. Our Miss Daisy's presence and pride came from within. So we renamed her Amazing Grace. She lived with us for two years, until she died of old age, and during that time she never ceased to astound us with what she was capable of doing.

Though we didn't know Grace's exact age, she and Lucky seemed contemporaries, and they had more than a long, hard life in common. Both hid their vulnerability behind a kind of bravado. And while both demanded—and received—respect, when I would hold them, they would both melt. In the end, they yielded their suspicion of humans, and craved to be loved and touched and kissed.

♥ ♥ ♥

I have a photograph of Lucky and Schultze on a brisk spring day wearing their matching sweaters, snapped during one of their daily walks. "Lucky, you're so handsome," I said, and as if on cue, he sat. Schultze scurried over and positioned himself right between Lucky's front legs. The two old boys look delighted, posing next to the pool as if on a photo shoot for *Esquire*.

Whenever Lucky wore his sweater, he lit up. But what he truly valued was what it represented—the fact that someone cared, that someone special looked after and loved him. Like Amazing Grace, he had waited a lifetime for that.

Mackenzie

Sandy was barking, but that didn't mean much. At Angel's Gate, that is like saying the refrigerator is running, or that the sun sets in the west.

Sandy, an ancient white shepherd mix, is, to put it mildly, a career barker. He barks when he's hungry. He barks when he's bored. He barks when someone is lying on a bed that he wants, or when someone is lying on a bed he *thinks* he wants. He barks first thing in the morning, he barks in the middle of the night. For Sandy, barking is as natural as breathing.

Sandy is a survivor. He came to us when the woman who had raised him from puppyhood was diagnosed with cancer and needed to sell her home to pay for her treatments. Worried that her twelve-year-old dog would be euthanized if she didn't recover, she brought him to us.

That was seven years ago. Today, Sandy is pushing twenty, and shows no signs of leaving anytime soon.

On this perfect June morning, Sandy was barking at Lucky, and for once he had a good reason. I had opened the sliding glass doors to the backyard so the animals could go in and out, and Lucky had positioned himself right at the threshold. As I unloaded the dishwasher, I looked at his hunched silhouette. Though he had gained twenty pounds since he arrived here, his ribs and vertebrae still protruded so pitifully that you could count them. Even with Ann's lovingly home-cooked meals, Lucky would never be fat.

Get out of the way, Sandy complained with his staccato woofs. *Get...out...of...the...way.*

Lucky studiously ignored him. Just as Sandy would be lost without his bark, Lucky would be lost without that doorway. It framed his world view. He spent hours there, surveying his new home, a vision of utter contentedness. He saw who had gotten into the tomato patch, who had eaten a bug. He craned his neck to see the pigeons that we had rehabbed and released, and had returned to perch on the lawn furniture, reluctant to say goodbye. He watched me splash in the pool and inspected my four-legged hydrotherapy clients as they exited, shaking the water from their fur.

Lucky's obsession with that doorway reminded me of my mother. She was a strong and determined woman who was very worried about how things looked to others. A post-office teller, over the years she was offered many opportunities for promotion, but she turned them all down because accepting them would have meant leaving her teller's window, and she didn't want to do that. She liked watching the world and its happenings from her familiar perch.

My mother lived vicariously through me. When I married my perfect husband at the tender age of twenty-one, she was relieved and elated that I was on my way to living a tidy, traditional life. But I was the opposite of my mother—I wanted to get out from behind the window and live life, not watch others doing it. Even as a ten-year-old, I remember asking her if she was sure she had taken the right baby home from the hospital. And after a dozen years of marriage, I realized I wanted something more than an immaculately decorated house and a weekly manicure. When I finally left my husband, my mother was furious. "What more could you want?" she demanded.

My mother died before I started Angel's Gate, but I know what her reaction would have been to what I am doing now: pure, unadulterated shame. Here was her promising daughter, throwing everything away to tend to a household of dying animals.

But from my "yes-ma'am" childhood, to my "perfect" marriage—the only thing that ever felt entirely and wholly right to me was the career path I had chosen. Nursing was something that came to me naturally, something I was good at, something that would always be a part of me.

♥ ♥ ♥

It took a baby raccoon named Mackenzie to teach me that sometimes my nursing instinct could take me too far. Mackenzie was the first raccoon I ever cared for. She had fallen out of her nest, and at five weeks old was so small she fit into the palm of my hand. I hand-reared her, and I named her, the only time I've ever named a wild animal; there is an element of domestication in the act of naming, and I believe that wild creatures are not intended to have that kind of relationship with people.

When Mackenzie arrived, though, I was new to wildlife rehabbing, and I was intoxicated by her. To be that close to nature, to nurture a wild animal, is so different from dealing with a domesticated creature. The energy is so primal. You really sense the vulnerability, and the consuming drive to survive.

I made a lot of mistakes with Mackenzie, the most serious of which was to create an emotional bond with her. But her antics were so playful and endearing, it was almost impossible not to. When I went into the pool, she joined me, splashing in delight. She rode around on my shoulder, her masked face bobbing near mine. Secretly, I wished we could keep her.

Once Mackenzie was a little older, she went outside to live in an enclosure with thirty other raccoons we were rehabbing. Slowly, she began to lose interest in us and to reconnect with her species. Still, when I came to the pen, she would gleefully climb on the wire, happy to greet me.

I didn't think of it that way at the time, but in a way I had stuck Mackenzie behind a post-office window of her own. Wild animals don't have time to reflect on life. They are too busy surviving. If a wild animal is injured and can't be returned to the wild, the ethical solution is to euthanize her rather than subject her to a life in captivity. When a longtime animal rehabber first told me that, I was appalled. But I've come to see the hard wisdom in it.

The best thing for Mackenzie would have been for me to detach myself from her emotionally and prepare her for her return to wildness. But it didn't work out that way. A distemper epidemic hit the local raccoon population, and soon it swept through the raccoons in our pen. Within days, only four had escaped it, and Mackenzie was one of them.

But a few days later, I noticed the telltale nasal discharge and coughing. Within hours, as the disease took hold, Mackenzie became lethargic, almost zombie-like.

I sequestered her immediately in the garage, and tried everything to save her. Herbs, homeopathy—nothing worked. And I knew that even if, by some miracle, Mackenzie did survive, she would be left with permanent brain trauma, and very likely epilepsy. She would be unreleaseable—relegated to a cage, glimpsing through the window the life she craved but could never return to.

Every animal that has come to Angel's Gate has been a teacher. The lesson I learned from Mackenzie was about the importance of freedom. On another level, I suppose, that is what death is: a return for every creature to the wilds of spirit.

♥ ♥ ♥

It seemed to me that Lucky, sitting at the back door, struck a perfect balance between my mother's limiting fear of the unknown and Mackenzie's unquenchable thirst for it. Unlike Mackenzie, Lucky was hardwired to live with and love humans, and being with us was a comfort for him, not a trap. And unlike my mother, he knew that it wasn't the picture-perfect view from the window that mattered, but the nature of your relationship with the very imperfect people and creatures in it.

After a few minutes Lucky grew tired and leaned against the door frame, but his eyes stayed glued on the yard. Summoning up their courage, a few of the smaller dogs scooted out past him, barely brushing his leg. If Lucky noticed, he pretended not to.

But Sandy was far too big to pass unnoticed. And it wasn't in his nature to even try. He was the center of his own universe, and he expected everyone else to make way for him.

Woof, woof, woof, Sandy repeated with irritation. *Get... out... of... the... way.*

Wearily, Lucky swung his massive head over his shoulder and looked solemnly at the irate, curmudgeonly shepherd. Lucky stared, unblinking, for what seemed like a full minute—precious time away from his beloved backyard vista.

And Sandy, sensing a stubbornness and resolve that matched his own, let out a final, tiny woof of protest, then walked away to find something else to bark about.

Brutus

Lucky and his lady, Ann
Spend their days holding hands,
An ancient soldier frail and weak
Who hardly ever speaks.
But oh, she loves him just the same,
And how he loves to hear her call his name
As she comes walking through the door.
He's never known love like this before,
But now he knows . . . now he knows . . .
That's how love goes.

As the last notes lingered in the air, Vic and I sat on the couch in our pajamas, clutching our coffee mugs. Lori, our houseguest, put down her guitar.

"Do you like it?" she asked shyly, pulling her robe around her.

I ran across the room and hugged her. That was answer enough.

I had met Lori a year before at a holistic conference. In the hotel lobby, I had heard a melodious voice, and couldn't help but follow it, past the reservations desk, past a row of potted plants, to where Lori was sitting in the lounge, strumming a guitar that she later told me she had named, of all things, Angel.

She put Angel down, and we got to talking. Like me, Lori had been a nurse, and she too had retired from that career to follow her dream—being a professional entertainer. It was a friendship just waiting to happen, and when I told her what we did at Angel's Gate, she offered to come and do a fundraising concert for us.

That was a year ago, and now Lori was back for her second concert. That morning, she had joined us at the breakfast table and, as she sipped her coffee, she watched Lucky quietly, basking in his presence as he was basking in the sun. It was October, and outside the sliding doors the fallen leaves rattled and danced in the wind.

Periodically, Lucky lifted his head and looked around distractedly. If he were human, he probably would have glanced at his watch.

"He's waiting for Ann," I said to Lori, who had seen the two together for the first time the night before.

Suddenly Lori jumped up from the table. "I'll be right back," she said, barely getting the words out before she raced back to the guest room.

When she returned twenty minutes later, she had a song. The Angel's Gate Song, inspired by none other than Lucky and the love of his life, Ann.

> *There is a place called Angel's Gate*
> *Where pain and suffering have to wait,*
> *Where life is given every chance,*
> *And crippled hearts can once more dance.*
> *And where they love you just the same,*
> *Where you love to hear them call your name!*
> *As you come walking through the door,*
> *You've never known love like this before!*
> *But now you know... Now you know...*
> *That's how love goes...*

Thrilled, I bought a big piece of poster board and hand-lettered Lori's lyrics on the shiny white expanse. Around the words I glued photographs of Ann and Lucky together. Now all that remained was to see Ann's reaction when she walked through the door for the concert later that night.

Throughout the day, we prepared the house for the festivities. We swept the great room, bathed all the animals, set out chafing dishes, and made a final round of the backyard to make sure all the poop had been scooped. Last, but not least, I gently placed a red bowtie around Lucky's neck, and fiddled with it until it was set perfectly straight: the dapper gentleman in him would demand nothing less.

❤ ❤ ❤

There's only been one other dog in my life who looked as elegant in a bowtie. He was a Rottweiler named Brutus, and the name fit. At 165 pounds, this overweight, unneutered eight-year-old had a head like an anvil and a stubborn streak to match.

Brutus came to us from an orthopedic surgeon who didn't know what to do with a quadriplegic Rottie: out for a walk with his family one day, Brutus had collapsed without warning on the street. The problem was two herniated disks, and the surgeon was reluctant to try surgery because of Brutus's age and the delicate location of the injury. The family wanted other options, so the vet halfheartedly suggested rehabbing

Brutus at Angel's Gate, though he didn't have much hope about the dog ever standing again, much less walking.

To say that physically managing Brutus was a chore would be the understatement of a lifetime. It took two people to move him anywhere. Though Brutus was incontinent, he was also fastidious, and he waited until we carried him outside in his cot before he urinated or defecated. And in addition to those frequent potty trips, I needed to get him into the pool at least once a day for hydrotherapy.

It didn't help that Brutus hated water. He had the intensity typical of a Rottie, and I'm sure that even before his injury he was a gruff customer. But, like Lucky, Brutus had no choice but to show us his gentle side. As we dragged him over to the pool and got ready to lift him in, he would growl, a low hum that sounded like an air conditioner in August. But as soon as the water enveloped him, Brutus relinquished control to me. As he bobbed in his life jacket, I slowly and meticulously stretched each limb. The part he loved the most was floating on his back— within minutes, he'd be snoring.

Initially, Brutus's family was hopeful about his prognosis, but I tried to temper their enthusiasm. An injury like his would take a long time to heal, if it did at all. I had hope, but no hard data to support it: dogs as severely disabled as Brutus rarely get rehab, so I had no idea what to expect. Brutus came to us in August; by November, he could move one paw—barely. He still couldn't hold his head up for any length of time, and he would have been more likely to recite the Pythagorean theorem than stand on his own four feet.

That wasn't much progress, and it certainly wasn't enough for Brutus's family, who lived in the city and couldn't keep him in this condition. Their only viable solution was euthanasia, they explained in a phone call, and as I hung up, I sobbed. Here was a dog who had lost everything—the use of his legs, his home, his family. How much more could he be asked to give? Besides, Brutus existed now only because of me. And I wasn't ready to call it quits.

I regained my composure and called them back. Would they sign a release form and transfer responsibility for Brutus over to me? Angel's Gate would rehabilitate him for free, I explained, and if he never got better, we would keep him just as he was.

Three long weeks passed. A few days before Christmas, the signed release form arrived in our mailbox. That was my Christmas present that year, just as Lucky's arrival had been several years before.

Winter had arrived, but Brutus couldn't afford to miss even one hydrotherapy session. So every day, Vic helped me lift him into the steaming hot tub on the deck, then waved to us from the toasty confines of the kitchen as I climbed in, my neoprene suit a sorry barrier against a winter that was one of the snowiest

I can remember. At the end of the hour-long soak, I'd have icicles hanging from my nose hairs.

With spring, the weather improved, but Brutus's progress was still unimpressive. After ten months of intensive therapy, he was able to lie like a Sphinx, chest down and paws out. That was it. But it was an improvement—before he could not even get off his side. So I decided to bring him along as my special animal guest to Manhattan's Plaza Hotel, where I was going to receive the ASPCA Founders' Award.

It was a formal dinner, and we dressed accordingly: I wore a white pantsuit with a silk sweater, Brutus was in his red tuxedo bowtie. The only way to get him into the hotel was to carry him in on a stretcher, and so I did, with Vic's help, my high heels wobbling. My arms felt like flan as I carried the immobile Rottie into the hotel lobby, but Brutus looked so handsome that people stopped us every few feet, wanting to pet him.

♥ ♥ ♥

Lucky looked just as handsome in his bowtie the night of Lori's concert at Angel's Gate. He waited for Ann in the first row in front of the stage, resting on a pile of pillows and blankets. When she walked in to the house and read the words on the posterboard, she cried. Then she made her way to the great room, and as she entered, Lucky's tail thudded excitedly against the floor. He sat with his head on Ann's lap while Lori sang the words that had taken her only a few minutes to write, but that would be with us for a lifetime: there wasn't a dry eye in the house. And as Ann stroked his head, Lucky nodded off, occasionally widening the slits of his eyes, wanting to get one more glimpse of his beloved before sleep came.

♥ ♥ ♥

For his part, on the night of the ASPCA awards, Brutus had left the Plaza, yawning luxuriously as we toted him back out to the car on his stretcher. I didn't know it then, but the relentless pace of our physical therapy had primed his body to make a comeback. It had just required his chowhound spirit to give him the motivation.

Two weeks after Brutus was carried out of the Plaza on a stretcher, and ten months after he had come to us, Vic set down a bowl of food for another dog, and Brutus shot up off the cot. It was that sudden, and that simple. Brutus was walking again.

Brutus hasn't made a full recovery, and he never will. He is still mildly ataxic, which means he walks around as if he's had one drink too many, stumbling and losing his coordination. But he is mobile enough to be able to run and hide from me when I try to get him into the pool for his hydrotherapy. And like Lucky, once he regained the use of his legs, he set about walking every inch of the house, inspecting his kingdom, and deeming it satisfactory.

At Angel's Gate, I always leave room for storybook endings like Brutus's. But the truth is that they are the exception, not the rule. Most of our paralyzed dogs will never walk, many of our dying dogs will not live to see the start of another year. I knew Lucky had already been with us for far longer than we could have hoped. And I knew we would have to start readying ourselves for the final words of Lori's song.

> *Where they honor the final phase of life*
> *Wrapped in love, somehow you're not afraid to die.*
> *And when you're ready to pass through Angel's Gate*
> *You just look up . . .*
> *And you will see . . .*
> *Your angel's face . . .*
> *At Angel's Gate . . .*
> *Angel's Gate . . .*
> *Angel's Gate . . .*

Juliet

I often think about Lucky's life, tied under that tree. How the days must have faded into weeks and years. How his neglect and mistreatment never blunted his love for people—how he could come to love us so effortlessly and naturally, when all he knew of humans for most of his lifetime should have taught him otherwise.

And I know that if I had come across him in that yard, I would have taken him away on the spot.

Lucky came to us the way many of our animals do, through a rescue organization that didn't have the resources to rehabilitate him, and figured his advanced age and health made him an almost impossible candidate for adoption. He was, in short,

a bad investment. Other animals are here because their own-
ers couldn't come up with the money to pay for their surgery,
or balked at changing diapers on an incontinent dog, or giving
daily injections to a diabetic cat. To save both time and money,
their solution is often euthanasia. Many times vets call me,
uncomfortable with the idea of "putting down" an otherwise
healthy animal, but professionally bound to follow the owner's
wishes.

You'd think that animals that are as broken, ill, and abused
as the ones that find their way to Angel's Gate should be easy
to save. After all, they are unwanted, and are considered bur-
dens or inconveniences by the people who are responsible for
them. But oftentimes it's a struggle to get them to relinquish
the animals. They insist on having their animals euthanized,
even when they know that a home waits here at Angel's Gate.
Many feel guilty and hopeless and fatalistic because they can't
envision a future for their dying or disabled animals. Or they
feel guilty about being unable or unwilling to devote themselves
fully to the animal's care.

I think another barrier to embracing our animals' imper-
fections comes from thinking of them as objects instead of
living creatures. I don't use the word "owner" to describe the
people that animals share their lives with: I could no more have
owned Lucky than I could the sky. Pet shops are among the
worst culprits in encouraging the idea of animals as "things"

to acquire as mindlessly as a Big Mac at a takeout window, and to dispose of just as quickly when they become inconvenient. And at Angel's Gate, no animal illustrated this better than Juliet the parrot.

Prolific breeders and hardy survivors, Quaker parrots are vociferous birds whose huge community nests can weigh up to a ton. When companion Quakers are released in rural areas, they strip fields of crops as they forage for food; in urban settings, they nest atop electrical poles, threatening to topple them. To farmers, utility companies, and most people who live within earshot of them, these dull-green birds are nothing less than winged vermin.

Yet, in those very same areas, pet shops sell Quakers. And people are willing to shell out hundreds of dollars for birds like Juliet, while a few miles away her relatives might be netted and killed because they were perched on a power line instead of inside a fancy cage.

Juliet was for sale at a pet store where I had been visiting a scarlet macaw. A career biter, the macaw had been returned to the store several times, and he persisted in trying to take a chunk out of anyone who came near. The teenagers who worked at the store only compounded the problem by banging on his cage as retribution, ensuring that his next reaction to humans would be even more dysfunctional.

The local parrot society had contacted us about bringing

the macaw to Angel's Gate, and Vic and I were visiting there every couple of days to see if we thought we could handle him. Because we knew that diet often dictates behavior—ever see a five-year-old after a sugar binge?—we'd stop at a nearby supermarket on the way there to buy him fresh fruit and nuts.

One day, en route to the movies, Vic and I stopped in for a quick hello.

"We can't let you see the bird," said the teenager on duty that day. "We're really mad at him."

After some prodding, I found out why: the macaw had attacked a young Quaker parrot that had flown onto his cage. Reaching upward with his powerful beak, he had crushed both her legs through the bars.

"She's all right," he added quickly. "We have her all bandaged up—she's fine."

But something told me she wasn't, and I insisted that he bring me to the back room where the parrots were housed. Finally he relented, and I followed him to a room marked "Employees Only" at the end of the store.

Inside the macaw was shrieking. Blood spattered the walls. And on the bottom of the Quaker's cage was a motionless bird, hemorrhaging through her bandages.

"I'm taking the Quaker," I said.

"I don't know if we can let you do that," the kid replied, slouching against one of the metal cages.

I scooped up the bleeding bird and walked out of the store as the kid followed after me. "Hey!" he yelled as we crossed the parking lot, "if she dies, bring back the carcass. We need it for credit."

I called an avian vet who tended to the battered bird, giving her an injection of iron and rewrapping her legs. She didn't tell me at the time, but she believed I was taking the bird home to die.

It didn't work out that way. After a few days, one of Juliet's legs turned black and fell off. The other leg had severe nerve damage, but one toe remained functional, and that, along with her beak, was all that Juliet needed to get around.

All our birds live in what used to be our family room. Cages line the walls and windows, and a computerized baby grand piano, a vestige of times when my nurse's salary allowed me to splurge, dominates one corner of the room. I had bought it back then so my children could have piano lessons. Nowadays, it trills out show tunes to accompany my frequent cleaning binges—I listen to *West Side Story* while I mop up a puddle left behind by an incontinent dog, or *Les Misérables* as I sweep up the peanut husks under a cockatoo's cage.

Flooded with sunlight, and so spacious it truly deserves to be called a "great" room, the bird room is a perfect sanctuary for our feathered residents. The soundproof French doors leading to the kitchen allow us to take an occasional break from the screeching and squawking, which are almost deafening at sunset. Visitors walk in and gasp at the rainbows of colored feathers and the knowing, blinking eyes of these great birds. Often they ask if they can take one home.

I always say no. When an animal comes to Angel's Gate, I make a promise that it will be a home for life. But something interesting happens when animals arrive here: I love and value and treat each one as if she were the most important creature on the planet. Then, strangely, my perception becomes reality: because I see value in an animal, other people do, too.

I doubt that Juliet would want to live anywhere else. Once she was completely healed, we put her together with a male Quaker who had been given up by his owner. They bonded immediately, and were so struck with each other that naming them after the Shakespearean lovers seemed inevitable. Today, Juliet hops around on one leg, clutching the perch with her one good toe, and has no idea that she's handicapped. As for Romeo, he doesn't care how many toes his Juliet has, or what she has to do to get from one place to the next. Some days, I wish humans were half as wise as my two little Quakers!

Jake

It was the best year of Lucky's life, and it was ending.

All summer, he had watched the poolside splashing as I swam with my canine patients, and had inspected the vegetables Vic brought in from the garden. In the fall, his eyes followed the leaves as they floated to the ground, and he "supervised" the volunteers as they raked them up.

On Christmas Eve, we had a party for him. We knew from his ASPCA file that he was fifteen that year, but since we didn't know his real birthday, we decided we would celebrate the day he had come to us a year ago. I baked special liver biscuits, and his friend Ann came over, and together we raised our glasses of apple cider to toast our good fortune at having had such a wonderful year with such a magnificent dog.

But as the year had faded, so had Lucky's sidekick, Schultze. He was getting on in age, and every week it seemed harder and harder for him to keep up with Lucky—and Lucky wasn't exactly a speed demon either. So we knew something definitely was not right. Most likely, Schultze's kidneys were acceding to old age and slowly closing shop. It was only a matter of time.

Lucky knew, too. In January when snow blanketed the backyard, he spent most of the time in bed, Schultze at his side. One day, Schultze refused to get up, and I started IV fluids to try to make him comfortable in the short time he had left. Lucky began to lick the little dachshund, over and over, as if kissing him goodbye.

I had often thought of Lucky and Schultze as crusty old men. Schultze was methodical and standoffish—"typically Teutonic," I used to joke. But there was nothing mean-spirited underneath that veneer of cantankerousness—Schultze was, for example, nothing like Jake, who was probably the angriest animal to ever walk through our door.

♥ ♥ ♥

A big old shepherd mix, Jake had spent his life in a junkyard until he developed a massive abdominal tumor. From puppyhood, he had been taught to be a guard dog, and he had taken the lessons to heart. Despite his adorably askew ears and cute face, Jake was 110 pounds of pure distrust and contempt. There wasn't much Jake liked—not cats, not other dogs, not people. We soon learned never to extend a hand to him—the consummate land shark, Jake would just as soon bite you as look at you.

Talk about special needs—this senior-citizen snapper needed to be given a wide berth in a house brimming over with animals. So I gave him the space underneath my desk, arranging a blanket for him between the Queen Anne legs.

We hung a "Beware of Dog" sign above Jake's head: sometimes we even hung it around his neck. We didn't dare get our fingers close to him, so we used a long pole to loop it over his head. We groomed him the same way, with a brush taped to an aluminum painter's pole.

Of course, Jake wasn't born violent or territorial—he had been taught very successfully by humans to bare his teeth and ward people off. He had made a career of being angry. Convincing Lucky, whose job had been to sit in a backyard and get beat up, that humans weren't all bad was a challenge. Convincing Jake was a near impossibility.

Still, we had to try. We offered him food. We tempted him with toys. We sat next to him in silent communication. Nothing worked. Jake stayed in his two-foot-by-five-foot sanctuary under the desk, watching the goings-on but refusing to be a part of them.

Jake lived at Angel's Gate for six months, much of it with his lip curled in a perpetual snarl. Accustomed to being powerful and formidable, the thirteen-year-old was failing, and it frustrated him. Even toward the end, when he couldn't get up anymore, he tried to bite anyone who came too close. It took two people to lift him, each grabbing an end of the wide blanket while keeping him at arm's length—literally.

It was an unseasonably balmy day in November, and Vic and I had just flipped a coin to see who would be stuck at the "head end" of Jake's blanket. This old dog had spent his entire life outdoors, and we felt the 70-degree day was too much of a gift to ignore.

Carefully we lowered Jake onto the lawn. Vic returned to the house to do some chores, and I sat down at a safe distance to keep Jake company.

"This is the deal—you're dying," I said to him after a while. "And before you do, I want you to know that humans aren't all bad."

Then, for the umpteenth time, I reached out to pet him. But instead of encountering the customary flash of teeth, I got...nothing. Jake actually allowed me to touch him, and I felt the softness of his fur under my hands for the first time.

"If I could just let you know what it feels like to be touched by a human, you might not be against it," I said softly as I petted him all over—miraculously, he was still allowing me to.

Wordlessly, I went behind him and lay down, cradling him with my whole body.

I stayed like that for an hour, my arm draped over Jake, caressing his chest and whispering in his ear. Then, as the sun went down and a chill crept in, we carried Jake back into the house and tucked him in under the desk. Elated at my breakthrough, I leaned down and extended my hand to touch him one last time. And then he did it: without warning, he bit me. Fast and hard, and without an ounce of remorse.

It was a painful lesson, but a valuable one. I now realize it was not my place to change Jake. It wasn't my job to make him love me. (I'm not even sure he liked me.) But I had found the one space and time in his life when he had allowed himself to be vulnerable. Maybe he was curious about what it was like to connect with a human being, and once that curiosity was satisfied he went back to his old ways. All I know is that the experiment lasted for just that one hour. It had never happened before, and it never happened again.

But that's all right: the whole purpose of Angel's Gate is to meet the needs of the animals in our care. Jake didn't want to be cared for in a loving way. He only wanted to taste human kindness, the way some of us might like to sample a too-rich dessert, and end up pushing the plate away.

What Jake really wanted to be was a guard dog, and he was one until the end. As he got weaker and weaker, I slept on a cot in the room with him, until he finally let go. Like most deaths at Angel's Gate, Jake's was quiet and peaceful—the ultimate contrast to his stressful life.

And Schultze's was no different. With Lucky at his side, licking him slowly and deliberately, the spunky dachshund left quietly, his little body slowly stiffening.

Though I hadn't heard from them in more than two years, I called Schultze's family to tell them he had passed away. As I hung up the phone, Vic's eyes caught mine.

"What's wrong?" he asked.

"They want Schultze back," I replied.

My hope had always been to bury Lucky and Schultze together. They had taken such joy in each other's company, and both had found love at Angel's Gate, with each other.

But I knew that the body is just a vessel, and it didn't matter ultimately where Schultze was laid to rest: I knew he would be with us in spirit, always.

Before his family arrived to take his body away, I cut a lock of hair from over Schultze's heart and put it in a tiny heart-shaped box. I knew what I was saving it for, but I didn't say it out loud. When it was time, Lucky would be buried with this little piece of Schultze. As for their spirits, I knew these two old soul mates would find each other again. Of that I was certain.

Dreamer

When Schultze died, Lucky mourned. You could see the weariness in his step, the somber look in his eyes when he lay on his bed by himself.

But he wasn't inconsolable—animals usually aren't. They grieve, but they also accept the inevitable. They don't cling or hold on to something that is impossible to keep. Lucky knew that Schultze's time had come to an end, and that was that.

But just as remarkable as the ability of animals to accept death is their ability to embrace life. Despite the pain and abuse of a lifetime, Lucky loved life more than anyone I've ever known. He continued on when most others would have given up. The racehorse breeders and trainers have a word for it: heart. And in its raw intensity, it will beat perfectly proportioned limbs and muscle-popping conditioning any day of the week.

Lucky's life had left a physical toll on him. I think people were drawn to him because he looked so fragile and weak, and they just wanted to protect him. But some of the animals at Angel's Gate have quieter wounds, buried so deep no one ever really quite finds them.

Dreamer was a greyhound who raced at the same Florida track where she was born. At the start of one race, just as the gate went up, she catapulted out of the start box, and her paw caught in her racing silks. Tumbling like a die cast by a high roller, she passed out on the dirt track and was carried off on a stretcher.

When Dreamer regained consciousness, she was seemingly fine, though a little unsteady on her feet. But her racing career was over. The track contacted greyhound rescue, which eventually placed Dreamer in what they hoped would be a permanent home.

But Dreamer's adoptive family soon returned her. Greyhounds are renowned for their rock-solid temperament and inherent docility—which is also, sadly, what makes them good candidates for medical experiments, since they never retaliate against their tormentors, no matter how much pain they inflict. But Dreamer was a dramatic exception: she had snapped at a visitor, and the family wasn't taking any chances that the next episode might involve a bite to a child.

So off Dreamer went to a foster home, where she flashed her teeth again. Dogs that bite are not considered adoptable, and the rescue group struggled over what to do with her. Meanwhile, the foster home was instructed to keep Dreamer kenneled and muzzled when she wasn't directly supervised.

Finally, one of the rescue workers took Dreamer to a vet who wondered if her aggression was linked to her racetrack spill. An orthopedic specialist discov-ered that Dreamer had a fractured and dislocated atlas—basically, a broken neck. Had she been x-rayed at the track, she would have been euthanized. But here she was, more than a year after her injury, not only alive but walking around, which, the doctor said, was a medical impossibility. Yet, except for a little head tilt, she looked like a normal dog.

Because Dreamer's shattered atlas had healed, the specialist didn't advise surgery, and instead recommended leaving well enough alone. But Dreamer wasn't healthy enough to go to a regular home. Hearing her sad story over the phone, I agreed to take her.

Now the problem was figuring out how to transport a dog

with a broken neck from Florida to New York. In the end, I flew down on a commercial flight and returned with Dreamer on Companion Air, a Florida-based airline devoted to transporting animals; they hadn't started operating yet, but agreed to fly us.

Back at Angel's Gate, I contacted my orthopedic vet, who concurred with the Florida specialist: since Dreamer was stable, the best thing would be to do nothing at all. He wasn't sure why she had snapped those two times out of the blue—perhaps every now and then when she moved her head the wrong way, it pinched a nerve. But he couldn't say for sure.

And we didn't care. We're aware of Dreamer's problem, and we live with it. We give her her space, and she hasn't worn a muzzle, nor has she snapped at any visitor, since the day she arrived. We're careful to keep her weight down and see that she gets regular exercise and, because her bone fracture has made her neck arthritic, she's on a regimen of nutritional supplements. Ironically, she's one of the gentlest dogs I've ever met.

♥ ♥ ♥

I tried hard to treat Lucky like a healthy, happy dog who had a long life ahead of him instead of a gangly geriatric who had outlived his life expectancy. But despite my cheerleading, he began to lose the hard-won weight he had gained over the previous year, and his movements grew slower, as if he were walking through a vat of invisible Jell-O.

Then one day, I followed him as he shuffled outside. As he stopped to mark near his favorite tree, I saw that the urine was tinged with blood. Before he had even returned to the house, I was on the phone with the vet. But deep down, I knew I didn't really need to make the call. I knew Lucky's body was shielding a quiet secret. All the vet would do would be to give it a name.

And he did. In March, three months after Schultze died and a year and three months after he arrived at Angel's Gate, Lucky was diagnosed with bladder cancer.

Mystery

I was poking through a bunch of forgotten files in my computer when I came across the letter.

I had never printed it out, much less mailed it to the veterinarian at the ASPCA who had saved Lucky by sending him here. But the question that had prompted me to write it still lingered. So I called the vet up, and after I told her the sad news about Lucky, I asked her the question that had always nagged at me.

"Why him? Why, of all the animals that you have, why did you choose to save *him*?"

"It was his eyes," she said. "There was just something special about him."

Sometimes it's easy to look at all the pain and devastation in the world and think that helping just one person, just one animal doesn't mean much. Every day I get phone calls about abandoned animals with special needs, and I can't take them all in. How do I choose?

I just do. It's that simple. I do what I can, when I can, and I don't dwell on what I can't do. There are simply too many animals to be saved, and I can't help them all. But I like to think of the story about the boy who was on the beach, furiously throwing starfish back into the ocean. "Why are you bothering?" asked a passerby. "You can't save them all. It doesn't matter."

"But I can save this one," said the boy, tossing another of the delicate sea creatures into the water. "And it matters to him."

I can't save every animal in need of help, either. But I can save some of them. And though I have plenty of deserving animals wash up on these Long Island shores, there have also been times when I have traveled halfway across the country to bring home an animal who has called to me.

♥ ♥ ♥

Mystery was a stray cat who just showed up one night at the suburban Chicago home of Nadea and Arlyne. A retired schoolteacher with arthritis so severe she walked with canes and sometimes used a wheelchair, Arlyne was a longtime family friend of Nadea's, and lived on the first floor of Nadea's spacious home.

By her own admission, Nadea was a dog person. And Arlyne had been terrified of cats ever since childhood. But there was something mesmerizing—and, well, mysterious—about the beautiful white-faced, long-haired cat who appeared one spring day on their deck. She wasn't matted or dirty, but if she had a home, she wasn't in any hurry to return to it. The cat followed Nadea as she walked their two Maltese dogs and, out of concern, Nadea started to feed her.

Soon the cat took up residence in the yard. As if to woo her new landlords, she began to leave trophies from her hunting excursions—a gopher tail here, a squirrel leg there. Waiting patiently by the front door, the cat would escort Nadea and the dogs on their walks and, one day, she surprised everyone— including, perhaps, herself—by jumping into Nadea's lap.

By then the two women had been won over by the cat they named Mystery. And the calico was very clear about wanting to join the household: every night she slept pressed up against the front door, as close to the inside as she could get. One day, with winter approaching and Arlyne's affection for the little cat overtaking her trepidation, they opened the door wide and brought Mystery in.

The two lost no time making Mystery feel at home. They constructed a comfy ledge by the window so she could see the creatures she no longer hunted. Noticing that Mystery followed behind when Nadea watered the houseplants, lapping water from the leaves, Arlyne concluded that this was how she must have found water in her wild days. Within a week, Arlyne bought Mystery her own tabletop water fountain.

But three happy years after Mystery had arrived in their backyard, the vet discovered that her kidneys were failing.

Almost overnight, Mystery became a very sick cat. The vet explained that she would need subcutaneous injections twice a week to keep her hydrated. Her kidney problems would only worsen, he noted, and that would require her to come into the office more and more frequently. Somewhere in his explanation, he tossed out the word "euthanasia." A second opinion from another vet echoed the first.

Arlyne and Nadea rejected the idea of euthanasia immediately. All that Mystery needed to keep her alive were injections a couple of times a week; but that sounded easier than it was. Mystery hated being in the cat carrier, and she hated the shots even more. When it came time to leave for the vet, she would duck under a big chair in the living room, petrified. When Nadea finally caught her, she would moan and hiss and cry. And after she returned from the vet's, Mystery would go back to hiding until it was time to catch her again.

After a few weeks of watching Mystery decline, Nadea read about Angel's Gate in *People* magazine; the first sentence of the

story began, "It's a mystery." Thinking this was an omen, and desperate
for a solution, she picked up the phone
and called me, hoping that Mystery
could find a home at Angel's Gate.

As I talked to both women, I could
feel their pain over the no-win situation: in providing Mystery
with the medical care she needed to live, they were destroy-
ing their little triangle of friendship. I was their only hope.

So I bought a round-trip plane ticket to Chicago.

Overjoyed, Nadea went into public-relations overdrive,
writing a press release and sending it to the local papers. When
I arrived at the airport a few days later, I was met at the bag-
gage claim by reporters and photographers, and Mystery's story
appeared on page one of the *Chicago Daily Herald.*

But, back at Angel's Gate, her illness soon stopped being
front-page news. I decided not to make a big deal out of Mystery's injections. Instead I'd sit in bed with her, snuggling and
watching television; she soon let me give her the fluids without any fuss. Eventually she stopped needing them. Switched
to a natural, raw-food diet, Mystery gained back her lost weight,
and transformed in an amazingly beautiful creature. I haven't
hydrated her in months, and she drinks water on her own, her
health problems resolved for the foreseeable future.

Mystery has been a permanent resident of Angel's Gate for

more than a year now, but Nadea and Arlyne still call periodically to check on her progress. At Christmas they sent a donation. And last Valentine's Day, Mystery sent me chocolates, though her handwriting looked suspiciously like Nadea's.

Even though Mystery isn't with them physically, Nadea and Arlyne are still connected to her emotionally and spiritually. They know that love isn't limited by geography.

Nadea and Arlyne's wisdom and compassion are qualities that usually are acquired with time and experience. But by age eleven, my little friend Timmy had a deeper reverence for life than most adults I know.

Tim was a sixth-grader from a nearby school district. When his class hatched four Pekin ducklings in an incubator, he asked his teacher where they would go after they outgrew the science project. The answer horrified him. After a very truncated life-span—Pekins are bred specifically to be plump and plodding, in anticipation of their eventual role as holiday dinner—the little quackers that he and his fellow students had lovingly raised were going to a slaughterhouse.

Tim decided on the spot that that was not an acceptable option. So he called around for days trying to find a refuge for the fledgling ducks. Finally he found me. He told me his sad story, concluding quietly, "Will you take my ducks?"

What do you think I said?

But when Tim arrived at Angel's Gate, driven there by his

dad, he didn't have the *four* ducks that he had described to me over the phone. No, he had *twenty-four* ducks! Not only had he called on all his classmates to round up all the other imperiled ducklings that had been reared in other classes, but he had created such an uproar at the school that the administration had vowed never to incubate any eggs, Pekin or otherwise, ever again.

Sadly, few of my other animals are as fortunate as Mystery or Tim's flock of ducklings. Plenty of animals arrive here orphaned or abandoned; we know they had families, but how they were separated or when their humans gave up on them is a mystery too.

Perhaps it's best that way.

Keshoggi

Lucky's cancer had worsened, but he refused to let go. He had found love, and who were we to tell him when he had had enough?

When the spring days warmed a bit, we took him outside and laid him on an inflatable mattress on the warm stone patio. He lapped the sunshine up thirstily, as if it were a fresh bowl of water. He was far too weak to walk, but occasionally he would lift his head and let out a deep, heartfelt bark. And I would poke my head out of the window and answer him.

"Good morning, my king!" I would shout through the open window. "You look so handsome today!" And I meant it— even when he was dying, there was a radiance about him.

Sometimes I would hear a faint growl coming from Lucky, and I knew exactly who he was talking to: it was Keshoggi, an Afghan-hound puppy I had taken in just after we learned about Lucky's cancer.

I was flipping through an old issue of *Redbook* at the veterinarian's office, waiting for my turn to bring in the three dogs I had with me for acupuncture treatments, when a stunning blonde walked in. She had a movie-star quality about her, as if she belonged on the stage set of a film noir instead of a plastic chair at the vet's office.

Then I noticed the dog. A nine-month-old Afghan puppy, he was all legs and hair.

"What a nice dog," I said, stroking his long, floppy ears. He unfurled his tail from its curlicue and began to wag it.

"I can't believe he's letting you do that," the movie star said. Periodically running her fingers through her hair and rubbing her lips together to assure the symmetrical distribution of her lipstick, she told me the story of the puppy she called Keshoggi. She had adopted him from a shelter at four months, and he lived with her, her boyfriend, and the boyfriend's ninety-five-year-old father in an apartment. She traveled often, and asked if I could recommend a kennel.

"I would be more than happy to board him for you," I said, bending down to air-kiss the handsome hound. As our eyes connected, he growled at me.

I wrote down my number for her, and didn't give it another thought.

When the phone rang a month later, it was the woman, this time with a more detailed story. She had made arrangements for him with a local boarding kennel because it was more convenient for her, but Keshoggi had lunged at one of the workers, and they had refused to take him. In truth, she admitted, this wasn't the first time he had done so: he had bitten two of her boyfriend's father's nurses.

"Do you want to board my dog?" she asked wearily, and braced herself for another refusal.

"Sure," I replied. "When?"

"Today—I'm leaving for Europe tonight," she shot back hastily.

When the doorbell rang a few hours later, it wasn't the movie star waiting on the other side of the door—it was the boyfriend. With his expensive car and foot-tapping impatience, he struck me as the kind of man who is accustomed to getting what he wants. And he wanted Keshoggi—who stood next to him, muzzled and cowering—out of his life. His father, he told me offhandedly, was a Holocaust survivor who had been attacked by a German shepherd in the concentration camp. He didn't like Keshoggi very much, and kicked him whenever he got too close.

I take in a lot of people's headaches, and I never know

what the truth is. But with Keshoggi, it didn't matter. It was love at first sight. I hadn't had an Afghan hound in the house since Phoenix died, and I knew that eventually another one would show up. Now it looked as if this was the one.

I removed Keshoggi's muzzle, took away the tranquilizers that had been sent with him, and gave him what he really needed: love. There was such a sadness about him, and I knew his aggression came from being afraid and striking out before someone struck out at him. At Angel's Gate for the first time, I think, Keshoggi was given permission to be a puppy. He ran around the backyard like a madman, confused when the older and sick dogs wouldn't follow him.

When he got too close, Lucky, though he was dying, still had enough of his old gumption to issue a warning growl, and Keshoggi bounded away as if he had been delivered an electric shock.

The movie star called me from Paris after three or four days, and I reported that I had ditched the tranquilizers, and that Keshoggi was getting along just fine with all the dogs and cats and people. "But it's a honeymoon period," I warned her. "He's on his best behavior."

A couple more weeks passed, and she called again, this time to tell me that I should put Keshoggi up for adoption because she couldn't return home with him. Her boyfriend wouldn't allow it.

"I'm not putting him up for adoption," I said. "If you don't want him, he can stay here."

Though his spirit has been broken, Keshoggi is young and healthy, and I suppose technically he doesn't really "belong" at Angel's Gate. Keshoggi's demons surface regularly. He still snaps unexpectedly at new visitors, and he is especially distrustful of children. Whenever he has to interact with unfamiliar people, we muzzle him, because we cannot take the chance that he will bite someone.

But Keshoggi will spend the rest of his life here at Angel's Gate. Why? Simply because I made a commitment to him, and I will keep it, whatever the inconvenience or difficulty. My house is filled with animals whose families have tossed them away because they no longer "fit in." If I were to abandon Keshoggi, would I be any different?

My answer to the Keshoggi dilemma is crystal clear to me. But at other times I struggle, as I have done with another puppy, a boxer named Samson.

Samson has a congenital deformity in which his joints are missing. His lower legs are useless appendages, and he "walks" on his elbows and knees, the lower parts of his legs flapping, like a marionette whose strings have gone slack.

His breeder in Indiana sent Samson to us when he was five weeks old. Now, at seven months, he is a third the size of his littermates, who each weigh more than sixty pounds. At a dainty twenty pounds, he is a dachshund-sized boxer, but he scrambles around the house gleefully, unaware of his disability.

I have sent Samson's x-rays all over the country, and there is one vet who thinks she might be able to reconstruct his limbs. It will require fracturing all of his bones, and a long recuperation period; and, because no one has ever tried this before, the outcome is far from certain.

To be honest, I'm not sure if I will go ahead with the surgery. A part of me says Samson deserves the chance to be a "normal" dog, running around the yard and jumping on the bed. But another part of me says he is perfect just as he is. In my mind's eye, I can still see the angry mother whose severely disabled son I tended to when I was a pediatric nurse.

"Poor Sean," I said to her sympathetically one day.

"Don't say that *ever* again," she replied fiercely. "Sean is happy the way he is because he doesn't know how to be any other way."

I was stunned—at how right she was and how wrong my assumptions had been.

I don't have all the answers to the dilemmas posed by the animals I take in, by any stretch of the imagination. I don't know why Keshoggi still refuses to trust people, despite the love and attention we give him. I don't know what the best solution is for Samson. But I did know, as I watched Lucky's sides heave on the air mattress, as his breathing grew more laborious and his time shorter, that with Lucky we had accomplished what we had set

Samson

out to do. We had given him love, and it had healed him. He was a living, breathing lesson in the power of faith. Lucky's faith that human hands would one day show him love instead of pain, that if he only gave some more, he would get it back in kind, was a beautiful testimony to the healing power of love.

And love, I know, is the best answer to most questions, no matter how complicated they are.

Josie

Ann was at the stove, her back turned to Lucky as she carefully cooked his steak. The pan sputtered as the thick red meat browned, and Ann rolled the pan from side to side, concentrating as the juice splashed back onto the steak, the biggest and best one she could find at the supermarket.

Lucky was in his bed, which he hadn't left for a week. At this stage of his illness, the only thing that moved were his eyes. They followed Ann's every motion, from counter to stove and back again. This had nothing to do with hunger: Lucky had stopped eating days ago, and the steak was no more tempting to him than a piece of cardboard. No, Lucky was only hungry for Ann—her attention, her voice, her touch.

It was late March, only three weeks after we had first heard Lucky's diagnosis of cancer. And today I could feel that he wanted to leave. *I am tired, so very tired,* his eyes seemed to say. *And I am ready.*

But there was something keeping Lucky here, despite his pain and weariness, and that something was Ann. Her love for him was so powerful, so all-encompassing, that it kept pulling him back from where his spirit was straining to go. When she walked through the door on this day, the one that I was sure would be Lucky's last, he perked up at the sound of her voice, and life and longing crept into his eyes like water lapping at the sides of a boat.

All of the animals at Angel's Gate are special, but some, like Lucky, commandeer you in an indescribably wrenching way: it's as if you share the same heart. And when their time with you begins to wane, your emotions can push aside a lifetime's worth of wisdom. All you want is more—one more minute, one more day, one more furry nuzzle, one more look into those knowing eyes.

We humans complicate death so much, making it something fearsome and mysterious. The animals know better. To them it just is what it is—an end and a beginning, a death and a birth. At Angel's Gate, our animals have taught us that death is just a normal part of life. We celebrate life for as long as we have it, and we do not rush to end it. But when death comes, we see it as another door through which we must walk to go to an even better place, and we gently bid them goodbye.

But Lucky was having trouble letting go. True, he loved the T-bone steaks Ann cooked for him, and he loved the long, luxurious rubs in that favorite spot behind his ears, but most of all, he loved Ann. He knew she wanted him to stay and so, even as every cell in his body told him that it was time to leave, he dallied, like a straggling guest at a party.

As the smell of the sizzling steak filled the house, a knot of dogs assembled at Ann's feet, but I knew they were wasting their time. Ann would never give them Lucky's steak, even if he wouldn't eat it. And I knew another thing: Lucky wouldn't die as long as Ann was there.

Sometimes the greatest gift we can give our animals is permission to leave. I write these words very easily, but I haven't always understood them that clearly.

♥ ♥ ♥

Every woman should have a special girlfriend, someone who will watch old movies with you on sleepovers, who will commiserate with you when yet another boyfriend runs your heart through a paper shredder, who will tell you when your mascara is running.

Josie was a ten-year-old, black-and-white Chihuahua who weighed barely two pounds. But in the flash of her wise eyes, the irreverent toss of her head, I saw a gal pal as vivacious and trustworthy as any I had ever met.

Josie's small size belied her outsized personality. Whenever I came home, a throng of dogs invariably assembled, barking and leaping and generally making good-natured fools of themselves, while the cats looked on in disdain. Amid this yelping pack would be Josie, weaving in and out of everyone's feet, most of which were large enough to crush her. If I didn't acknowledge her quickly enough, she would make her way to the end of the crowd, cock her head just so, and look at me as if to say, "Where have you been? And why didn't you take me with you?"

Josie was intent on being a Thelma to my Louise. Whenever she saw me searching for my car keys or putting on my makeup, she'd trot over to my pocketbook and start barking at it, and she wouldn't stop until I scooped her up and plopped her into my bag. That's where she traveled, her head resting contentedly on my wallet, serenaded by the rattle of a Tic-Tac container.

Josie had cancer, said the rescue group that gave her to us: there was a malignant nodule on top of her apple-shaped head. But they hadn't noticed her enlarged lymph glands, which suggested that the cancer had spread.

When Josie arrived, I set up a bed for her in my daughter's old bedroom—now a consummate teenager, Dantae had moved into the basement, where she had more room and privacy. So Dantae's room was now a nursery for toy dogs: most slept in portable cribs, and the smallest ones lounged on folding doll beds. With the pastel-colored baby furniture and stuffed animals, I wanted this room to be joyful and hopeful, not somber and depressing.

Despite her illness, Josie was as sunny as that room, which, frankly, she didn't spend much time in. Within days of arriving, she was encamped on my bed, refusing to sleep more than a few inches away from me. All of a sudden, I had another magnificent, totally devoted animal in my life. She had just appeared one day, and the instant she did I knew she owned me.

Josie went everywhere with me, largely because no one wanted to be with her when I left her behind. She was insufferable, whining and pacing and moaning as if she had just lost her best friend, which in a way she had, if only temporarily.

For four months, Josie accompanied me on all my errands. When I enrolled in school to train as a veterinary technician, she rode shotgun until the professor asked me to stop bringing her. ("It might set a precedent," he explained apologetically.) Twice a week, I did hydrotherapy at a specialty veterinary practice, and Josie came along too. There she became so well

known that when we walked down the hallway, the staff was more likely to greet her than me.

Then one day Vic called me on my cell phone in the middle of class. Respecting the professor's request, I had left Josie behind. Vic got right to the point. "Josie is dying," he said, in his maddeningly blunt way.

"Excuse me?" I whispered incredulously. "She was running around just yesterday. You don't just die." But when I got home, I could see that Vic hadn't overreacted. Josie was going in and out of consciousness. I tested her blood sugar, and the reading was so low that it didn't even register.

I rushed her to the emergency clinic, but the vet on call was baffled. He had no idea what was wrong with her, but it was clear that she wasn't going to get better and recover. Her cancer had made sure of that.

"Where are we going here?" he asked me gently but pointedly, setting down her chart with the depressing test results.

I knew he couldn't "fix" Josie, but that's not what I was hoping for. "All I want is more time," I said. "I haven't had her long enough."

Four days later, when the clinic called to say that Josie was grumpily snapping at staffers, I knew I had my wish. She was coming home.

And home is where she stayed for the next four months, except when we were out on one of our jaunts. As we drove around, I'd talk to her about everything—my big plans for Angel's Gate, my fears that we were down to the last $200 in the checking account. And she'd listen, with that half-cocked head of hers, as if to say, "don't worry, everything will be fine."

Then came the day that I was leaving the house, pocket-book slung over my shoulder. "Come on, Josie," I called to her. "You want to come?"

Lying down in the office room, Josie lifted her head off her paws, then laid it back down again.

Over the next few days, Josie grew weaker. I knew that if I brought her back to the clinic, the talented doctors could resurrect her again. But I also knew that if I did that, I would be doing it for me, not for Josie. She had already graciously stayed around for longer than her worn body should have allowed her. And this time she was so ill that she might linger for weeks at the clinic. Josie never wanted to be far from home—far from me—and I decided that I wanted her to be at Angel's Gate when she died.

The call from Vic came in the middle of another veterinary technician's class. I excused myself to answer the phone, and Dantae was on the other end.

"Mommy, you have to come home," she said, her voice so serious I felt like someone had punched me in the chest. "Josie is going to die."

Dantae has said many times that she can't see herself

ministering to animals the way I do. She prefers to advocate for them from afar, signing petitions and joining in marches. But she has grown up watching me, and as Josie lay dying, she instinctively knew what to do. By the time I arrived, Dantae was giving her subcutaneous injections and oral sugar water, which is exactly what I would have done had I been there. Even in my frantic concern, I felt a swell of pride in my daughter.

I only had a half-hour with Josie before she slipped into a coma. "It's all right," I whispered to her. "You can leave." And as much as I wanted Josie to stay with me, I wanted more for her to be free of her pain and to go on to whatever awaited her. She did just that before 5:00 a.m., as the sun streaked the sky.

♥ ♥ ♥

Lucky's time was coming, too. We all knew it, Ann as well as anyone.

Finally, the night he died, well after midnight, Ann began to gather her things. She must have started for the door and come back a half-dozen times to see if Lucky wanted anything else. Yes, his blanket was tucked nice and tight. Yes, he had had a mouthful of water, but wanted no more. Yes, he had the freshly pressed pillow under his head.

Still unconvinced that Lucky had all that he needed, but unable to think of anything else, she finally left. Lucky followed her with his eyes and, once the door clicked behind her, he closed them, weary but content.

Once, when a newspaper reporter visited Angel's Gate to write a story, she walked through the door to find me in the hallway in a whirlwind. Betty, a dog with mammary cancer, had collapsed, and I was carrying her on a stretcher to the rear bedroom that I use as an ICU, holding an IV bottle aloft like the Statue of Liberty.

It made for a dramatic story, but it's not how animals usually leave us at Angel's Gate. Most of them die the way they lived out their final days—peacefully, quietly, naturally.

Lucky was no different. He died at 3:00 a.m., fifteen months after he came to Angel's Gate, and just a few hours after Ann had left her bedside vigil.

Lucky

These days, nobody sits in Lucky's doorway at Angel's Gate. Unimpeded by the big black figure who once sat sentinel there, the dozens of dogs who live here now move freely between the kitchen and the backyard. Sandy, once Lucky's most vocal critic, long ago found something else to bark at.

No one sleeps in Lucky's old spot either. We've made sure of that by pushing the kitchen table back to where it stood before he arrived: it just wouldn't feel right to have another animal in his place.

After Lucky died, Ann still came back every week. He's buried out back, in what we call the Angel Garden, within earshot of the splashing of the pool where he so contentedly watched me swim and listened to the crunch of Vic's shovel as he overturned the rich soil of the vegetable garden. A cement statue of an angel overlooks the graves of animals who have passed here, and Ann has blanketed Lucky's patch of earth with color-coordinated flowers as she murmurs to the dog who taught her so much about loving and being loved.

Though it seemed as if he lived here forever, Lucky was with us for just over a year. It's a miracle that he lived that long, but it's not a surprise. After he found a home where he was loved, Lucky simply refused to leave it before he was ready, and his spirit convinced his body to hold out just a little bit longer.

Not all of the animals who come to Angel's Gate feel as strongly as Lucky did about staying for as long as they can. Some die hours after arriving here. And a handful know they are never meant to stay.

We had an injured swan who fit the last category. She had been found in the middle of the road, probably hit by a car. Her wing seemed functional, so the likelihood was that she had injured her pelvis. From Mackenzie the raccoon I had learned my lesson about keeping an emotional distance from the wild animals I cared for, so I never named the swan. Since she was too frail to face the winter weather outside, we lodged her in a logical place—in our bathtub. Admittedly, sharing your daily ablutions with a wild bird was a little off-putting at first, but she was a great conversation piece for guests.

When spring came, the swan joined the other birds in the pony pen, and nature called to her, loud and clear. She would practice her runway takeoff, racing from one length of the property to another, flapping her wings portentously. Still, she was with us for more than a year as she built up enough strength to resume her wild life. Vic saw her fly away: he heard a flapping, and said it was like watching a jumbo jet take off.

We never saw that swan again. Thinking she might take up in a more secluded area nearby, we searched the woods behind the house, but there was no trace of her. I have no idea where she ended up. A wild animal's instinct is so strong—they know what they're supposed to do, and they do it.

The swan is gone, but in another way, she is not. She is forever a part of this special place I have created, and her story is permanently woven into the web of love that we are spinning here.

Hundreds of animals have lived and died at Angel's Gate in the twelve years since I established it. It's grown from a handful of dogs to more than two hundred animals at any given time. And though many of them have left us physically, I can still feel their presence.

I still have the sweaters that Lucky and Schultze wore so proudly, but I haven't tucked them away in a special memory box. Instead, I let the house's current canine residents put them to good use. It's the memories that are sacred to me, not the things.

But I do keep a lock of hair from each animal, and save it in a small pouch. Native American tradition says that if you have a lock of hair from departed loved ones, you will stay in communication with them. I believe this, too: I still talk to some of my animals, like Phoenix, my Afghan hound, long after they have passed. It was her recovery from distemper that taught me how to believe in myself. I find myself talking out loud to her now just as I did when she was alive, especially when I am unsure about something, or when I need to make a major decision.

Phoenix was hit by a car after she snuck out of the house one day. I don't think I've ever experienced that kind of pain. "Please," I remember thinking after we found her motionless body on busy Pulaski Road, "I need to know that you're okay."

The night after Phoenix died, I had a dream about her. I don't usually remember my dreams, but this one was so vivid that I remember every detail. It was a serene forest scene, and Phoenix was walking along a crystalline brook. She was sniffing the water, and it was so incredibly peaceful. The dream touched each of my senses: I could smell the forest, feel the coolness of the water, see each droplet on the smooth stones of the brook.

I reached out to touch Phoenix. I wanted to stroke her head and tell her how much I missed her. But I couldn't reach her—she was with me, but not physically.

When Vic woke me, my pillow was soaked with tears. It was the most wonderful dream I have ever had, and I don't think I've ever been more sure, or more assured, that there is life after death—that where we're going is an incredible place, and that animals are there and are a very big part of it.

Do I talk to Lucky? Of course I do, and I feel his presence around me just as strongly as I did when he slept on his beloved bed in the kitchen. I talk to Lucky when I am angry, or when the people around me have let me down. He reminds me, with his gentleness and stoicism, how to be patient, and how to believe in the goodness of people, despite everything.

The word "animal" comes from the Latin word "anima," meaning "soul." And I truly believe, through my work at Angel's Gate, that animals show us every day what is truly important, and what we often forget: that we shouldn't get caught up in the trivial. That to love is to share yourself deeply, and unconditionally. That life should be joyful, even when it is ending. And I believe with all my heart that creatures like Lucky leave this earth when they've completed their work with us. They are the greatest teachers we will ever know; at Angel's Gate the door is always ajar, hoping they will accept the invitation to come in and share their wisdom with us all.